THE SCOTCH

THE SCOTCH

JOHN KENNETH GALBRAITH

with Illustrations by

Samuel H. Bryant

McClelland & Stewart trade paperback edition published 2002

First published in hardcover in Canada by
The Macmillan Company of Canada 1964

Trade paperback edition, with new Introduction and Afterword,
published by Macmillan of Canada 1985

National Library of Canada Cataloguing in Publication Data

Galbraith, John Kenneth, 1908-
The Scotch

First ed. published 1964.
ISBN 0-7710-3257-9

1. Scots – Ontario – Elgin (County) 2. Elgin (Ont.: County) –
Social life and customs. I. Title.

FC3095.E44Z7 2002   971.3'340049163   C2001-903453-9
FI059.E4G3 2002

We acknowledge the financial support of the Government of Canada through
the Book Publishing Industry Development Program
for our publishing activities.

Portions of this book appeared in *Harper's Magazine* and *Maclean's*.

Typeset in Goudy by M&S, Toronto
Printed and bound in Canada

McClelland & Stewart Ltd.
The Canadian Publishers
481 University Avenue
Toronto, Ontario
M5G 2E9
www.mcclelland.com

1 2 3 4 5   06 05 04 03 02

For Arthur Schlesinger, Jr.

Contents

Foreword

Books can be broken broadly into two classes: those written to please the reader and those written for the greater pleasure of the writer. Subject to numerous and distinguished exceptions, the second class is rightly suspect and especially if the writer himself appears in the story. Doubtless it is best to have one's vanity served by others; but when all else fails it is something men do for themselves. Political memoirs, biographies of great business tycoons and the annals of aging actors sufficiently illustrate the point.

As I warn the reader this book falls unmistakably into the suspect category. In recent years I have found myself combining periods of intense activity with long intervals of functional idleness – journeys when I could not sleep, intervals between engagements, speeches and conversations that required only a show of attention. It was during these odd moments, for my own pleasure, that I wrote this book.

The story of the Scotch involved no very taxing ideas. I suppose, also, it involved a certain pleasant nostalgia. But I would not like this to be thought in any measure a personal memoir. I am more than normally resistant to the idea of advancing age and I intend, so far as possible, to have no part of it. I would rather see this manuscript join Carlyle's in the fireplace than encourage anyone to hope that I am now turning to personal history and retrospection.

This is the kind of story where memory plays one tricks. I have checked names, places and events. But records are sketchy and it was forty years ago. I can only hope that I have been spared. Here and there, as the reader will guess, I have deepened a shadow or sharpened a line or contributed one of the folk-tales of the community. Here and there too I have changed the name of someone who is still living or of some family about which it seemed better to be tender. Among the Scotch such rearrangement of names involves considerable risk, for in exonerating one clan you automatically implicate another. I hope this will be understood and forgiven. The rest is as it was.

I am grateful to my sisters, Alice Galbraith and Catherine Galbraith Denholm, and to my cousin, Ida Galbraith, for getting me various records which I needed to refresh my memory, and to the Elgin Historical Society and Museum for lending me maps and documents. I suspect that some of my old friends and neighbors will feel that I could have spared the reader some of the less agreeable scenery and ignored some of the less enchanting personalities. The instinct to improve on history is strong among them as others; I have encountered references to Colonel Talbot which contend that neither alcohol nor profanity ever passed his saintly Irish lips. I would remind my old friends that, as Oliver Cromwell instructed for himself, portraits are best done "roughness, pimples, warts, and everything." To retouch is to sacrifice plausibility and, more than incidentally, readers too. And I doubt that in the aggregate this account will be thought damaging.

JOHN KENNETH GALBRAITH
Newfane, Vermont
September, 1963

Introduction
to the Second Edition

Encountering my books on a shelf in our living room, I have a very different reaction to the various jackets and titles. Some give me a feeling of discomfort, even pain; they recall the hard months and years of writing. Such is my response to various of my efforts on economics, and I yearn to believe that the feelings of those who have read them are not the same.

But there are some books that I see with mild pleasure. The writing was a relaxed and enjoyable experience; there was no grave suffering. In this benign company, along with a novel on high government policy misadventures in Central America and a history of the great stock market crash of 1929, both of which I greatly enjoyed writing, there is this book, *The Scotch*.

As I told in the original foreword, I wrote it as an antidote to tedium. I did not tell that it was while I was in India as an ambassador in the early 1960s. An ambassador's job, as someone has said, is much like that of a pilot of an airplane – there are hours of boredom and minutes of panic, it being the latter, presumably, for which ambassadors (as also now airplane pilots) are needed. I filled in the sometimes endless hours by writing, and it was thus that I wrote this book. The material, most of it, was amply and pleasantly available from memory. There was no deadline; I could take as much time as I wished, for time was what I was seeking to consume. Sometimes I wrote while listening to speeches. One cannot read while attending a speech of barely endurable length, but one can write. All, including the speaker if he stoops to notice you, think you are taking notes, especially if you remember to look up occasionally with a smile of well-simulated understanding and approval.

As the writing was rewarding, so was the aftermath. The reviews were good; any author who tells you that he doesn't pay attention to his reviews is either James Joyce or a consummate and unconvincing liar. Surprising to me were the numerous letters from across the United States and Canada from persons who had grown up in other farm communities with a strong ethnic orientation – Germans, Norwegians, Swedes. I had, they all said, described *their* early lives and surroundings. I had assumed, needless to say, that the Canadian Scotch were *sui generis*.

Engaging also was the reaction of my home community. On this I was at first cautious. Somewhere I had read that Stephen Leacock, after publishing the *Sunshine Sketches* about his home town of Orillia, was not for a long time allowed to venture back. When the Canadian Broadcasting Corporation asked if I would appear in a documentary that they were contemplating on the countryside and people I had described, I asked my sister, Catherine Denholm, living then in Elora, Ontario, to go and assess the local terrain. She reported back that all was fine: those who were mentioned in the book did not approve, those who were not mentioned did not approve. This being a normal Scottish reaction, I went ahead with the show. In the onetime barroom of the McIntyre House which I describe in these pages a local habitué told my television host that he "hadn't heard that anyone liked the book." Then, conceding that it was generally truthful, he went on to inquire as to "who in hell would want to hear the truth about a place like this?" Rather forthright even for the Scotch, I thought. The librarian of the Dutton public library in those days told *The Toronto Star* (as my memory serves) that she had purchased copies under protest. She had earlier, out of loyalty to a local boy, bought a copy of my *The Affluent Society*, and no one had taken it out. She explained that then, like so many authors, I had thought, with *The Scotch*, to retrieve with something sensational.

This was not entirely favorable, but, if I might digress, I have not always been even that fortunate in the response of the friends and associates of my youth. After I left the agreeable precincts in Elgin County of which I here tell, I went on to study agriculture, in particular animal husbandry, at the Ontario Agricultural College at Guelph, Ontario. Once and, I'm sure, since a distinguished institution, in my years it had fallen on evil times. Then a political outreach of the Ontario Department of Agriculture with a vague affiliation with the University of Toronto, it had sunk, as have other centers of learning, into lethargy and repetition, sustained only by a militant assertion of institutional virtue and vigorously voiced demands for student and faculty loyalty. Sadly lacking was the scientific motivation that elsewhere on the continent had served agriculture so well. That graduate work and advanced degrees were a qualification for research and teaching was a thought that was universally and even indignantly rejected. As the students were deeply anti-intellectual, so also was the faculty. After graduation I wrote a series of articles which detailed these deficiencies for *Saturday Night*, the distinguished Toronto journal of public affairs and good works; they were not well received at the O.A.C.

Then, with the passage of time, my alma mater became a university – the University of Guelph. I was forgiven and invited back to receive an honorary degree. The citation read to me by the President the night before the ceremonies described me as "Our most distinguished graduate." Reflecting on the sad state of the institution in my days, I thought what I heard was "Our only distinguished graduate." That, I concluded, would not have been at all accurate; numerous others have also survived their earlier education, including Thomas H. Jukes of my generation, a major modern source of knowledge on vitamins. But, I discovered, not everyone was in a benign and forgiving mood. The next morning, as I've told in *A Life in Our Times*, I rose early and walked over the familiar, shaded, shrub-grown and singularly beautiful campus. It all seemed fresh from heaven. Presently I met a professor from my day, a man of great years but vigorous aspect, who recognized me immediately from thirty years before. He stopped, shook hands and said, "I see by the newspapers, Galbraith, that they are awarding you one of those honorary degrees."

I bowed in recognition.

He shook his walking stick in a menacing way and said, "Well, if I had my way, they'd be taking away the degree you already have."

Three years ago, as I write, my class celebrated its fiftieth reunion. I thought of returning to join the survivors in the now-nostalgic glow. Then it occurred to me that I might meet my old professor again. Wisely, I think, I decided to forgo the risk.

The Scotch, to return to this book, had many translations and was particularly well received in France. I rejoiced to think of Parisians over their coffee on the rue Montparnasse savoring the quality of life of the idlers in Dan McBride's store in Iona Station. It did well, as publishers say, in Japan; there were, indeed, two Japanese editions. I've always wondered what an educator in Tokyo might think of S.S. No. 4, Dunwich Township, or the perverse pedagogical skills of Thomas Elliott, Old Tommy, of the Dutton High School.

The British edition, I might note, was called not *The Scotch* but *Made to Last*, the reference being to the highly durable material that covered the faces of my fellow-clansmen in Ontario. Modern British custom requires that the Scotch be called Scots, the word Scotch being reserved for the whisky. Our Ontario etymology is the more accurate. Anciently we were called the Scotch; it was thus that Dr. Johnson spoke of us when he went to the Highlands with Boswell. On English usage no one can wisely say that Dr. Johnson was wrong. When Penguin published a paperback in Britain, the book was entitled *The Non-Potable Scotch*. A truly repellent compromise.

By all more recent generations in Iona Station, Dutton and Wallacetown, the original stir has, I'm told, long since been forgotten. I am quite forgiven. For this I am grateful and believe it could be partly the product of a very happy accident of geographical proximity. Only a few miles north and west of Dutton lies the pleasant town of Thamesville. This is the principal setting of one of the indispensable works of fiction of the twentieth century, the Deptford trilogy of Robertson Davies. A Canadian writer, Davies belongs to all countries; every month or so some friend or neighbor of mine in New York or Cambridge tells me with the air of a recently successful Arctic explorer that he has come across Davies's work and wonders if I am similarly fortunate and blessed. Compared to Davies and Deptford, the story of Dutton, Iona, Wallacetown and their neighbors is a small achievement. But perhaps it prevents these villages, as compared with Thamesville, from being wholly ignored and forgotten. Perhaps it is also for this, along with the absolution inherent in passing and advancing years, that I am redeemed.

JOHN KENNETH GALBRAITH
Cambridge, Massachusetts
December, 1984

THE SCOTCH

I

An Uninteresting Country

The upper shore of Lake Erie extends east and a little to the north from the mouth of the Detroit River in a very flat arch. The arch has a little of the shape of an overpass spanning a very wide road. The actual shoreline is not much to see; for great distances it consists of a nearly vertical bank of clay a couple of hundred feet or so in height at the base of which is a narrow sand and gravel beach. Streams and inlets are few for, as the result of an illogical arrangement of the local terrain, the principal drainage for much of the land north of the lake is provided by a stream that runs parallel to the shore before it turns off north to flow into Lake St. Clair. The lake itself is not wonderful; on the horizon it is gray and blue but inshore the water is often rather muddy.

The land that lies back of the lake struck me even as a boy as being rather uninteresting. Other children of which one read had streams to patrol and mountains to climb and some natural curiosities such as caves or springs. We had none of these. A spring was only a muddy hole where the cattle watered. One brook ran in a dull way from the end of a tile drain just beyond our farm to the lake five or six miles to the south. It had water in it only for a few weeks in the spring and after especially heavy rains. After 1920, when we rebuilt our house, we were warned that it carried the overflow from the septic tank. The only available hill could be climbed in a matter of four or five minutes.

This peninsula which juts down between Lake Erie on the south and Lake St. Clair, Lake Huron and Georgian Bay on the north is very flat. Our part, indeed, was once a lake bed and the waters as they receded took with them all topographical interest. Nor did they leave it uniformly productive. The two buttresses of the Lake Erie arch, Essex and Kent counties across the Detroit River from Detroit and Lincoln and Welland counties across the Niagara from Buffalo, are very fertile. Fruit, vegetables, beans and tobacco flourish. But at the apex of the arch where I was born the soil is sometimes rather sandy, gravelly or poorly drained or otherwise inhospitable. However, there are superb stretches of deep black earth and these are mixed up more or less at random with the poorer land. And soil quality does not lend itself to dogmatic categories. The desolate sandy stretches which once went unwanted and almost unfarmed have been found in the last forty years to grow very good tobacco. It is a great mistake, incidentally, to imagine that tobacco is a heat-loving plant which matures only under a subtropical sun. This is a myth perpetuated by the tobacco ads. It is not believed by men who know tobacco best.

2

In the year 1803 a young Irish nobleman, Colonel Thomas Talbot, arrived at the apex of the arch at the precise point where the stream that originates in the aforementioned tile drain runs into Lake Erie. Here there is a minuscule break in the clay bank where a very small boat could be moored. This smallest of harbors was given the name Port Talbot and has ever since remained innocent of commerce. But for fifty years a rude manor house on top of the promontory was the headquarters of the Colonel. It was called Malahide Castle after his ancestral home and was the capital of a vast fief which had been awarded by the English crown to the Irish aristocrat for no discernible reason.

The land in this seigneury was densely covered with hardwoods – maple, beech, ash, oak, hickory, elm and ironwood. It was also the hunting ground of a few Indian tribes of negligible interest and distinction. About a hundred and thirty years ago, this land was settled and cleared. The settlement was strongly encouraged by Colonel Talbot who believed that he had a bargain which entitled him to two hundred acres for each settler established on the land, fifty of which was to go to the settler and a hundred and fifty of which was to reward the Colonel. The claim was doubtful but never effectively disputed, and it increased his original stake of some five thousand acres approximately twelvefold.

As settlers, Colonel Talbot preferred Englishmen: "My advice," he wrote a friend, "is that you should, as much as possible, avoid placing Highland Scotch settlers . . . as of all descriptions they make the worst settlers on new roads –

English are the best."[1] Highlanders, however, were the
ones available; they were being driven from their crofts
by sheep farming and the pressure of poverty, reasons which
were later improved to include the search for liberty, opportunity and political independence. And while the Colonel
thought ill of the Scotch, this was apparently in a competition that excluded the Irish and all other races except the
English. None of the other Colonel Talbot wanted at all. He
settled the Highlanders in dense communities where they
could communicate with each other in Gaelic, and hoped
for the best.

This, for him, was not altogether good. The Colonel was
Irish, aristocratic, eccentric, irreligious and often drunk,
and he was in possession of land that the Scotch believed
they should own. The first five of his sins his settlers were
willing to leave to the later judgment of a righteous God.
The ownership of the land was a more urgent matter. They
bought it, and though the price was modest, they never
ceased to protest.

The Talbots have long since disappeared. The Colonel was
a bachelor and his estate passed to his nephew, Colonel
Richard Airey. Colonel Airey was recalled to England and
to the colors in 1852, and sent on to the Crimea where he
was the subject of one of history's most awesome military
misfortunes. His and no other was the name on the order
that launched the Light Brigade. In comparison with such
towering incompetents as Lord Raglan when he served as
aide or Lord Cardigan who led the charge, it is doubtful if

---

[1] C. O. Ermatinger, *The Talbot Regime*. St. Thomas, Ontario: The Municipal
World Limited, 1904, 106.

the Colonel was much to blame. But he was never seen again at Port Talbot. Nor were others of his family.

3

By the time Colonel Talbot was answering to his Maker and Colonel Airey to his board of inquiry, the forests had been cleared away and burned or used to build frame houses with steeply pitched roofs, sometimes with wood fretwork under the gables, which were painted white with green trim. Often they were painted only once. Sometimes, in spite of the abundant wood, the settlers built square plain houses of white brick. Barns and outbuildings stood back of the house and, except in the rarest instances, were never painted at all. The forests did not quite disappear. Some swamps and gravelly tracts were not worth clearing. And at the back of each farm it was customary to continue a woodlot from which fuel and a little timber and in some cases maple syrup could be obtained. With the passage of years, these little forests have become thin and attenuated, often only a little more than a dense fringe between the fields. In the autumn when the leaves are gone, the countryside has a stubbly appearance rather like that of a man who has shaved in poor light with a very bad razor.

Yet it would be wrong to think of this as a land without beauty. On the contrary, I remember it, and quite accurately, as having a breathtaking loveliness. The difference is that this country does not flaunt its beauty everywhere and always. It is condensed both as to time and place. On a dozen winter mornings, the snow was deep over the fields and fences and sat in great patches on the evergreens in the yard. The purity of color was matched by equal purity of line. Even the steep roofs of the houses disappeared under a white mantle, with somewhat of the architecture of an English thatch curving gently out from the eaves and up to the ridgepole. Sun was not good for this landscape; it brought back a certain hardness of line, and even on the coldest days it destroyed the snow on the surfaces that were protected from the wind. But a full moon turned everything into a shimmering fairyland. On such nights we went skating at Gow's gravel pit and came home in subdued wonder at what we saw.

Then the snow became old and used, and the mud and steaming manure piles and derelict machinery showed through. But there were other moments – one of them when the apple trees blossomed and the grass was rich and green against the newly seeded land and another when the oats and mixed grain stood in shocks and the green had given way to bleached gold. The maples provided their special moment of grandeur in the fall.

In what remained of the woods, the spring brought thick patches of violets and forget-me-nots and a little later of wild phlox. A hilly stretch of land a half mile or so from our house was covered with sumacs. Every three or four years, circumstances favored blackberries and one picked them for hours under a bright green and red canopy of sumac encountering at intervals one's neighbors similarly engaged. I cultivated a reputation as an attentive and diligent picker, for it provided me with a passport to this paradise. Near the Lake is a little church and churchyard, and down a draw a few hundred yards distant one has a view out on the water. Here Colonel

Talbot and his retainers are buried. We were taught, as a matter of tradition, to regard their resting place with detached repugnance. They had not yet been forgiven for owning the land. This is also a small but beautiful place.

4

As the country was settled, small hamlets appeared. The English guided the larger political life of the community so the larger political subdivisions had English names or commemorated Scottish aristocrats. Elgin County was for James Bruce, 8th Earl of Elgin and 12th Earl of Kincardine, Governor-General of Canada 1846–1854; Aldborough, Dunwich, Southwold and Yarmouth townships were after their English namesakes. But the Scotch had their way with the microeconomic places – Iona, Wallacetown, Campbellton, Fingal, Crinan, Glencoe, Port Bruce, Cowal. Most of these were merely a corner where some individual, more enterprising or more averse to manual labor than the rest, had started a store which had then been followed by a blacksmith and, less frequently, a tavern.

In the early seventies, the railroads arrived. The short way between Buffalo and Detroit lay across the Ontario peninsula; problems of international transit of goods and people which would have caused endless difficulty in the twentieth century were worked out more or less automatically. The trains simply ran out of the United States, through Canada and back in again. The Canada Southern Railway, later the Michigan Central and later still the New York Central, was laid out a few miles north of the Lake. For a few brief years

the shoreline of the Lake had been an axis in the simple
geography of the land. One went down to the shore and
took ship to the outer world. But always the lake front was
rivaled by the roads, execrable though these were. And with
the arrival of the railroad, the Lake became part of the back
country. One went to it once or twice a year for picnics.
Occasionally a hot summer evening was relieved by a rush of
fresh cool air and people spoke of the lake breeze. But many
who lived not three miles away never saw the Lake at all.

Every six or eight miles along the railroad, where it
crossed a road, the railway company built a station. For a
while, at least, no village on the railroad failed to flourish.
And no trading center off the railroad ever did again. In
time, the railroads went into decline and the highways
came, but by then the pattern was set.

5

By the latter decades of the last century, this countryside
was curiously complete. The towns have not changed much
since, the farms only a little more. One of the better traveled
of the old roads, known as the Back Street in the other days,
has become Queen's Highway No. 3. At the apex of the
arch, it lies midway between the Lake and the railroad. It
has its own hideous roadside commerce but it has never
attracted the solid traders away from the older municipalities on the railroad. Population has not exploded; nor have
people been extruded. But it is not my purpose to write of
this community as it is today but as it was forty years ago
when I knew about it as a boy. I mean to give a true picture

of life in the Scotch-Canadian community in the early decades of the century. I am writing about it largely to amuse myself and because it is a story I can tell from memory and put down as I travel over India in an airplane, or in odd moments between diplomatic engagements, or while pretending to take notes on long-winded speeches, or to which I can turn my thoughts as I stand in endless reception lines, or as I seem to listen to visitors who have come to pay their respects. This latter compensation I would happily forgo. Most people who come to pay their respects to an ambassador wish really to listen to themselves talk. I try not to compete with them by listening too.

As just noted I am engaging in this exercise in social anthropology principally for my own benefit. Others may wonder why they should concern themselves with the manners, customs and behavior of the Canadian Scotch, commonplace or curious, in this particular region at this particular point in history. I confess that this question has also crossed my mind. I can only issue a reasonable warning. If anyone is in search of serious economics or grave politics or if he is short of either time or money he should leave this book in the bookstore or lending library or, having bought it, petition at this point for the return of the purchase price. For others the financial risk can presumably be absorbed. And it is my experience, at least, that few things require so little time as to close a book and put it permanently away.

II

The Scotch

An effort was once made to have the road on which we live called Argyll Street, as an attempt was also made to have the second road to the north called Silver Street. But the community had a strong preference for blunt nomenclature. The road to the north ran through light, sandy soil. It continued to be called Starvation Street even though it was said by some that the name had an adverse effect on land values. Our road was once also an unfavored stretch. The adjacent concessions had been settled first and the sows of the early settlers had taken their litters back to our neighborhood in search of mast. It came as a result to be called Hog Street. In an effort to retrieve something from total inelegance, the Dutton *Advance* had added an extra "g" but Hogg Street was the best that was ever done with it.

Hogg Street is in Dunwich Township some five or six miles from the Lake, and it runs parallel to the shore for some six miles from the Currie Road to the Southwold Township town line. Not even in the Western Isles are the Scotch to be found in more concentrated solution. Beginning at the Currie Road were first the McPhails and Grahams, then more Grahams, the McFarlanes, the McKeller property, Camerons, Morrisons, Gows, Galbraiths, McCallums, more McPhails, more Morrisons, Pattersons and among others the McLeods. Along the way were the Gilroys who may not have been Scotch and a man by the name of Malone. He had moved out from town in very recent times, it was said for his health. But Hogg Street was not exceptional in its commit-ment to the Highlands, and many parts of the township were much more specialized as to clan. To the north, around a hamlet called Cowal, nearly everyone was named McCallum. The Campbells were similarly grouped around another minute village bearing the not inappropriate name of Campbellton. One or two roads were occupied more or less exclusively by Grahams. In the larger towns, those of four or five hundred people and upward, one encountered a measure of racial diversity. Along the Lake, a few families of Irish extraction fished and supported a small Catholic church. And a few pros-perous farmers on the immediate shore traced their ancestry to the disgruntled Tories who came to Canada after the American Revolution. In Canada the Tory émigrés are called United Empire Loyalists, and it is known that they migrated out of affection for the King and a deep commitment to per-sonal liberty. Elsewhere there was a scattering of English and Irish names. But nearly everyone was Scotch. Certainly it never occurred to us that a well-regulated community could be populated by any other kind of people. We referred to ourselves as Scotch and not Scots. When, years later, I learned that the usage in Scotland was different it seemed to me rather an affectation.

2

Gogol once observed that there are "many faces in the world over the finish of which nature has taken no great pains, has used no fine tools, such as files, gimlets, and the like, having simply gone about it in a rough and ready way: One stroke of the axe and there's a nose, another and there are the lips, the eyes gouged out with a great drill, and without smoothing it, nature thrusts it into the world saying: 'It will do.'"[1] A stranger, on encountering one of our neighbors, would have rightly concluded that he had been fashioned in the manner described by Gogol, although with some additional attention to the durability of materials.

Our Scotch neighbors might be tall or short, stocky or lean, although most of them were unremarkably in between. But it was evident at a glance that they were made to last. Their faces and hands were covered not with a pink or white film but a heavy red parchment designed to give protection in extremes of climate for a lifetime. It had the appearance of leather, and appearances were not deceptive.

This excellent material was stretched over a firm bony structure on which the nose, often retaining its axemarks, was by all odds the most prominent feature. Additional

---

[1] In *Dead Souls*, ch. 5.

protection, though it may not have been absolutely essential, was provided for most of the week by a stiff-bristled beard. The story was told in my youth of a stranger who, in a moment of aberration, poked one of the McKillop boys on the jaw. He would not have been more damaged, it was said, if he had driven his fist into a roll of barbed wire. In any case, he was badly wounded. Our older neighbors wore a mustache. This was no clipped nailbrush but a full-flowering piece of foliage which grew and straggled and sagged at the ends as nature had obviously intended. In natural shades it might be black, red or gray. However on many of our neighbors, as the result of an informal rinse, it came out a rich tobacco brown.

On Sundays and at funerals, a Scotchman presented himself in a pepper-and-salt suit or sometimes a solid black, high laced shoes with broad toes, a stiff collar and a four-in-hand tie with the knot falling some distance away from the collar button. The man always looked smaller and more shrunken than his clothes, perhaps partly because it was considered sound economy to buy things a little on the large size. During the rest of the week he seemed a good deal more at home in his attire.

On superficial view, a man's working garments changed little from season to season. The basic components were high-bibbed overalls of blue denim, a blue work shirt and a blue denim smock with steel buttons. These faded steadily and rather agreeably with wear and eventually stabilized at a light sky blue, at least when clean. In the winter more garments – a waistcoat, sweaters, woolen trousers, fleece-lined underwear – were added underneath. (Heavy outer clothes, while they were put on for such sedentary tasks as driving to

town, lent themselves poorly to active toil.) As spring
turned to summer, the nether garments were shed while
the external covering and appearance remained the same.
However, a few clans continued to believe that the Canadian
climate was not to be trifled with. Although sweaters, vests
and the second pair of pants were discarded, it was considered safer to wear the heavy underwear right through. All of
us had heard the story of two elderly and childless neighbors
of ours who had the affectionate custom of going each year
to the Lake for a picnic. While the roast chicken, pickles,
pie and cold tea were being put out on the cloth, the
husband always went up the bank to bathe. One year he
returned downcast; he had lost his vest. A joint search
failed. But the following year he returned rejoicing.

"I hae found it, Jean!"

"Found what, John?"

"My waistcoat, Jean. 'Twa under my undershirt."

3

An enduring problem among the Scotch was that of personal nomenclature. As I have noted, a certain number of
the clans transported themselves to Canada in bulk, or, in
any case, reformed their ranks quickly on arrival. McCallums,
Campbells, Grahams and McKillops were exceptionally
numerous. That so many had the same surname would not
have been serious had they not so often had the same
Christian names as well. To call a son something other than
John was to combine mild eccentricity with unusual imagination. And even an unusual imagination did not normally

extend beyond Dan, Jim, Angus, Duncan or Malcolm. A fair proportion of the people we knew were called John McCallum. The John Grahams and the John Campbells were almost equally numerous.

The Scotch eliminated the danger of confusion by giving everyone a nickname. The parents having failed, the neighbors stepped in. The nickname might turn on some feature of a man's farm or location; most often it was inspired by some prominent personal trait. Since an unpleasant trait invariably makes a stronger impression than an agreeable one, the nicknames were usually unflattering and often offensive.

There were Big Johns and Little Johns and once there had been Wee Johns, but this form had gone out of use. There was also Black John and Johnny Rua, the latter being Gaelic for red and referring not to politics but to beard and complexion. More regrettably there was (or within recent memory had been) a Lame John, a Dirty John, a Lazy John, numerous Old Johns, a Bald John, a Nosey John and a Piggy John who was named for the number of, and his own resemblance to, his livestock. Most of the McCallums were Presbyterians; one who was not bore the proud name of John the Baptist.

The Scotch often tagged people with offensive nicknames even when they were not needed for identification. In later years I knew a boy whose parents had named him R. (for Robert) S. McTavish. The McTavish were a small clan; no further identification was necessary. But it pleased everyone to take advantage of the initials and call my friend Arss. The Scotch often commented on this practice of giving people disagreeable names. Those who had somehow escaped had no objection. Those who hadn't were very glad to see others suffer.

4

In all sophisticated societies, nothing is so nearly a social absolute as cleanliness. And nothing serves so universally as an index of character and worth. In a rich country, poverty, when combined with cleanliness, becomes respectable. "They are poor but very clean." In an underdeveloped country, regular bathing serves as an offset to an inadequate Gross National Product. "They haven't much money but they are clean and tidy." In the United States even few intellectuals are socially so secure that they can afford a gamy smell. For Madison Avenue, this has been a rich source of reward.

In 1837 one Mrs. Jameson, the wife of a judge of the province and a Frances Trollope of her time and place, visited Port Talbot and the Scotch settlements and reported on the state of the inhabitants. She was especially impressed by "Their clannish attachments and their thrifty, dirty habits – and also their pride and honesty." They had not changed appreciably by my time.

Our neighbors lived close to the soil and close to their livestock. Inevitably traces of both clung to them. Nor could everything be attributed to external influences. Men worked and perspired, and a nightly bath was highly impractical. Water would have had to be hauled and heated; anyone taking a bath pre-empted the kitchen, the one warm room in the house, which was needed by other people for other purposes. And a bath didn't do much for personal daintiness without a change of underwear. A daily change would have required a much larger investment than most of our neighbors would have thought reasonable, and the laundry involved would have been an intolerable burden. Better a mildly malodorous husband than a dead wife. The sensible compromise adopted by our neighbors was to clean up once a week. This was accomplished on Saturday night before going to town and it meant that a man remained in fairly good condition for church the following day. This modest and practical standard was, however, rigorously enforced. Failure to conform subjected a man to adverse comment. Two men are talking in the town of Dutton as a third approaches.

"Watch it Mac, here comes Andy Leitch!"

"Yeh, I see. The air is a mite blue behind."

"Wish there was a breeze. They say Andy's had no bath since he fell in the sheep dip."

"You're right, lad. Scratch the 'Le' of a Leitch and you have it."

5

But overgeneralization is the enemy of science. If the Scotch had certain resemblances in texture, attire and aroma, they otherwise displayed a pleasing diversity of personal traits. A sense of humor was not their most prominent feature but some, like our next-door neighbor Bert McCallum, were very amusing. They were not, as a rule, easily aroused to anger but occasionally one encountered a man, or a woman, who had the reputation of a hot temper. Few were belligerent and most were pacifist. During the First World War, when young Canadians were volunteering enthusiastically for euthanasia on the Western Front, the Scotch regarded the whole enterprise with reserve. They did not think the slaughter ennobling or especially necessary; more surprising, perhaps, they had instinctive misgivings about the men who were in charge. On both points they anticipated by some decades the judgment of historians. Yet, when inspired by alcohol, a Scotchman became very combative. In our community, a man did not get dead drunk but fighting drunk. The resulting battles were part of our folk history.

Some characteristics were specialized as to family or clan. Thus, the Camerons were very prolific. Sons and daughters married young and had children with celerity. This was also true of many of the McCallums. The McKellers, by contrast, had ceased to marry, and the local clan had only a few more years to survive. The Galbraiths a generation earlier had shown the same tendency. My paternal grandfather was a member of a family of seven. Only three married and these three couples, six in all, produced a total of only five children. The literature of celibacy is silent on the position of those who do not get born. To anyone who has only narrowly made it, the point is not without interest.

Differences in the size of family were related in considerable part to a sharp difference of opinion on the economic role of offspring. The Camerons in my time regarded children as a valuable earning asset. Only the minimum amount of money need be spent on their improvement. The marginal cost of getting and preparing an additional pair of hands thus being small, the more the better. This doctrine required that girls work as well as boys, and the Cameron girls worked with a will. In our case, as with quite a few other clans, education was deemed necessary. This cost money and, much more important, it greatly delayed entry into productive employment. (Proponents of the other system also felt that the individual so educated too often left the farm or that he returned with an exaggerated view of the possibilities of substituting mental for manual labor.) Whatever the merits of the two systems, where education was favored, the number of children had to be curtailed, and that was the accepted practice.

The total avoidance of marriage was not so explicitly defended by an economic rationale. There is no doubt, however, that it reflected the prudent tendencies of the community which extended not infrequently to the question of whether a wife was really economically essential. The families of bachelors and spinsters, which were a commonplace in our neighborhood, had presumably decided in the negative.

This calculation is not yet obsolete. A few years ago a Hollywood press agent was looking for a family of bachelors to publicize a film called *Seven Brides for Seven Brothers*. After an international search, he found seven unmarried brothers a few miles from Hogg Street toward the Lake. It would have been a logical place to look first.

III

Of Love and Money

The virtue and marital fidelity of our neighbors, from all outward appearances, were impressive. And more penetrating study would not have altered the impression. No one had ever received a divorce or asked for one. No one knew anyone who had been divorced. This was partly because until after World War I, there was no divorce law. What God had wrought in Canada, man could put asunder only by a special Act of the Canadian Parliament. Each year a certain number of Canadian couples did petition for such special legislation but they were much richer and far more willing to spend money for their personal peace than any of the rural Scotch.

In most countries where it is difficult to dissolve a marriage the community comes to take a rather tolerant view of informal recombinations where these obviously add to happiness

or even pleasure. Thus, the Italians, who have no divorce law, have gone far to perfect arrangements which make one unnecessary. The Scotch resorted to no such expedients. A tall and stalwart Highlander who lived very near our place had once been unfaithful to his wife, an almost incredibly unattractive woman, to the eventual impregnation of a maiden who lived a mile away. The baby, so it was said, was brought home in a red bandanna handkerchief and in any case was tolerantly reared by the wronged wife. By rough calculation from the age of the issue of this unblessed union, it all must have happened about 1890. It was still a lively subject for conversation when I was in primary school in 1919. No other instances of infidelity were immutably a part of the local lore.

Among the unmarried, the standards of deportment, by what were unquestionably the standards of the community, were equally high. To father an illegitimate child was to sacrifice one's citizenship for some years. The effect on the mother was more disastrous; if, thereafter, she married at all it would be to someone who was permanently devoid of position – a hired man, a man who drank, or at best someone with fifty acres and no alternative. We did not speak of shotgun marriages for firearms were not much known in the community; a boy who was compelled into marriage as the result of pregnancy was described as having put his part-ner "up a stump." This was also a serious social setback and though it would eventually be forgiven or forgotten it would be a rewarding topic of conversation for many months. Years before, one of the notably energetic McCallum boys was courting one of two sisters of the same name. (No suggestion of incest or inbreeding can be implied. The McCallums were

so vast and dense a clan that, in the absence of an exceptional willingness to travel, marriage within the clan was
inevitable.) An adventuresome type, he sometimes visited
his beloved by climbing up on the summer kitchen and into
the bedroom that she shared with her sister. When danger
in the shape of the senior McCallum threatened, he would
crawl into bed between the girls. By the worst of luck he got
the wrong girl pregnant. Though he promptly married her
and the McCallums were good farmers and intelligent and
public-spirited people, he was celebrated unfavorably by
the local historians for a long time and only gradually did the
adventure come to redound to his advantage.

2

In many cultures obloquy attaches to unlicensed intercourse,
especially if it becomes, in one way or another, a matter of
record. This is rarely sufficient to prevent it. Thus the continence and fidelity of the Scotch call for additional analysis.

More must be attributed to the absence of opportunity
than would first be imagined. There was no place, literally
none, where a questing husband could take an interested
wife and go to bed. He couldn't visit her house when her
husband was away for the reason that husbands were rarely
if ever away for as much as overnight. In any case, a man's
horse and buggy were as firmly identified with his personality as his nose, hair or gait and they would be seen passing
down or up the road or tied in the yard. In the center of
Katmandu, the capital of Nepal, is a temple and around all
four sides of it couples engage imaginatively in copulation

for all eternity. (One talented woman rewards two well-endowed and highly aroused lovers simultaneously.) A visit by a couple to the McIntyre House in Dutton would have been almost equally unreticent.

Unmarried affection encountered similar barriers. The girl's dwelling was filled with parents and siblings and thus unavailable to anyone less adept at second-story operations than the aforementioned McCallum. Resort to the barn, the classical arena of bucolic love, was an outright admission of intent. Also it would have been regarded by the better or even the average class of girl as rather vulgar. The couple could go riding together; chaperons were unknown and boys and girls, engaged or otherwise, went anywhere together. This, however, was allowed not out of liberalism but from a knowledge of the Canadian climate. In winter a cutter lent itself to lovemaking only at the cost of extreme contortion and an occasional chilling exposure. The alternative was a snowbank. Things were not appreciably more agreeable in the autumn on the frozen ground, in the spring in the mud or in summer under the onslaught of the mosquitoes. Chastity was everywhere protected by a vigilant nature. With closed and heated automobiles, things have doubtless changed but that is only conjecture based on a general view of human nature.

3

Something had also to be attributed to the uncompromising Calvinism of our upbringing. We were taught that sexual intercourse was, under all circumstances, a sin. Marriage was not a mitigation so much as a kind of license for misbehavior and we were free from the countervailing influence of movies, television and John O'Hara. Among the rougher element of the community, after the weather, the wisdom of selling cattle and the personality of the schoolteacher had been touched upon, conversation would often be taken over by one or another of the acknowledged masters of salacious detail. However, in contrast with other cultures, no one ever boasted of his own exploits, presumably because there was no chance he would be believed. More often a shy or especially puritanical participant would be accused of fornication with some highly improbable lass. Interest would center on the way he denied it. The charge would then be repeated, and coupled with more graphic, though even more imaginary detail, and a pleasant hour or two would thus be whiled away. Members of the more prestigious clans never participated in such pastime. In our family we would have been visited by a Jovian wrath had it been known that we even listened. The mere appearance of my father at a neighborhood gathering would turn the conversation back to crops.

An important feature of an austere education in such matters is that it need influence only one of the two people involved to be fully effective. And uncertainty as to the state of conviction of the other person, plus the moral consequences of miscalculation, can be a powerful deterrent. One such experience had a durable effect on me.

At some time during adolescence, I encountered a novel by Anatole France which made unlicensed sexual transactions, especially if blessed by deep affection and profound mutual understanding, seem much more defensible than I had previously been allowed to suppose. It was summer and I was deeply in love. One day the object of my love, a compact golden-haired girl who lived on Willey's Sideroad, a half mile away, came over to visit my sisters. They were away and we walked together through the orchard and climbed onto a rail fence which overlooked a small field between our place and Bert McCallum's. Our cows were pasturing on the second-growth clover in front of us. The hot summer afternoon lay quiet all around.

With the cows was a white bull named O.A.C. Pride, for the Ontario Agricultural College where my father had bid him in at an auction. As we perched there the bull served his purpose by serving a heifer which was in season.

Noticing that my companion was watching with evident interest, and with some sense of my own courage, I said: "I think it would be fun to do that."

She replied: "Well, it's your cow."

4

But I think most of the virtue of the Scotch was to be attributed to the fact that love for a good woman (or bad) was not the only ruling passion. There was also love for money.

One indication was the respect which was accorded to money in everyday conversation. People do not speak lightly about the things that they hold dear. On occasion, at a threshing or of an evening at Bert McCallum's, the same rough-spoken clansmen to whom I have referred would consider the ability of a well-to-do middle-aged neighbor to satisfy the demands of his young, vigorous and healthy wife. There might be jovial suggestions of the need to lend him, figuratively, a hand. But no one would ever dream of bringing up the man's bank balance or of voicing a wish that he might enjoy that. Such things were sacred.

The ordinary farmer referred to his wife, whatever her age, as "My auld woman" or "My auld lady." These terms did not necessarily imply dislike or disrespect; like the terms "dear" and "darling" in more refined communication they were neutral. But no such casual reference was ever made to money. No one spoke of "jack" or "dough" or "lettuce" or "long green." When it came into the conversation, as it often did, it was referred to respectfully as money or dollars.

This was, I think, pure love. Some have always wanted money for what it would buy. Some have wanted it for the power it conferred. Some have sought it for the prestige it provided. The Scotch wanted it for its own sake. Money in this community conferred no power. And while a good bank balance unquestionably enhanced a man's self-respect, he certainly did not think enough of the prestige it provided ever to dream of admitting to its amount. Two techniques for accumulating assets have always been in some measure in competition. One is to earn money; the other is to avoid spending it. Our neighbors enthusiastically employed both. When he visited Scotland with Boswell, at the time when the migration to America was getting under way, Dr. Johnson observed that "A man, who keeps his money, has in reality more use from it, than he can have by spending it."[1] With this the Scotch continued to agree.

---

[1] James Boswell, *Journal of a Tour to the Hebrides*. Thursday, 26th August (1773).

5

The passion for money as money reinforced continence and fidelity in several ways. For one thing, faithful and chaste behavior was the least expensive. Within the family, children were comparatively costless but an illegitimate child could call for cash. A boy married when, with his auld man's help, he could make a down payment on a farm and manage the rest under mortgage. The compulsions of an unpremeditated pregnancy would badly upset this timetable. Many might think that it made better financial sense to leave the community for a year or so and the girls, knowing this, had an inducement to chastity. Sex education among the Scotch depended largely on experience, instruction by the learned of one's own age and informal deduction based on the behavior of breeding stock. But most parents took occasion to tell their young of the serious financial risks which were inherent in yielding to what they unhesitantly called the baser instincts.

More important, the love of money meant that as other passion receded, a man's life did not become less meaningful. Marriage for life, especially if decided on by the principals, is an exceedingly hazardous arrangement, as all experience shows. The line between love and lust is one that participants can neither draw for themselves nor on which they can accept counsel. And love is less than durable. If it is deemed central to life, its disappearance means either that life is totally barren or that a remedy must be sought in adultery, divorce and replacement or, should the culture allow, bigamy, polygamy or polyandry, all of which are in the area of the original disaster where, to some extent at least, one failure presages another. The love of money meant that a man's emotions were reliably engaged until the day he died.

6

Yet the Scotch were also notably wary of any person who allowed his emotions to rule him. As many people expect a woman to love men without being a nymphomaniac, so the Scotch expected a man to love money without being a miser. Excessive preoccupation with economy would not cost a man his membership in the society but it could be the cause of considerable adverse comment. One of the great McKillop clan was always known as Codfish John. (Dried codfish was the cheapest form of protein available in the winter months. It was universally detested and a man who fed it to his family, hired hand or the neighbor who, in accordance with the custom of the community, might drop in unannounced for a meal, was suspected of stinginess.) Many stories were told of Codfish John's economies. His wife did not average one new dress a decade. Her only recreation, and similarly that of the family, was a weekly trip to church in a democrat behind a plow horse. All community festivals – the Wallacetown Fair, the Caledonian games, the Christmas concert – were denied to his family; they were believed to implant ideas of extrava- gance even in the not excessively impressionable mind of a McKillop. On Christmas Eve, so it was said, John lit the lamp and entertained his bairns by making rabbits on the wall. The entertainment did not continue long because of the expense of the oil and the possible wear on the wallpaper. When he was finally being lowered into his grave at Black's

Cemetery west of Wallacetown, it was said that he lifted the cover of the coffin and handed out his coat, waistcoat, pants and undershirt. That was not widely believed. But he did warn his wife to take up the parlor carpet before the funeral.

Interestingly, it was always said of Codfish John, as of anyone else who was excessively frugal, that he was "very Scotch."

IV

Husbandry

Lives are measured off and the passage of time given meaning either by the rotation of the earth on its axis or by its more gradual but much grander movement in orbit around the sun. For urban dwellers, the teeming hordes of Southern California and those who live in the tropics, it is the succession of day and night that is important. But the fortunate people of the planet, although the blessing is not universally recognized, are those who live by the seasons. The seasons have an unpredictability and an individuality which appeal both to the sporting instinct and the very great need for simple topics of conversation:

"It looks like a late spring."

"Early winter this year."

"Nice autumn."

The seasons also work a great and magical change in the landscape – there is far more difference between a Vermont farm in the summer and the same farm in the winter than there is between San Diego and São Paulo. This means that people who live where the seasons are good and strong have no need to travel; they can stay home and let change come to them. This simple truth will one day be recognized and then we will see a great reverse migration from Florida to Maine, New Hampshire and on into Quebec.

Although the climate of southern Ontario is not especially severe, the seasons have a very satisfactory accent, and this is sharpened by the cycle of agricultural operations. Here I must digress to another poorly understood point.

In modern times, especially in the United States, notions of natural beauty have been extensively compromised by the Cult of the Wilderness. The justification for this cult is plausible enough. Men have seen the squalor of the places where people live or travel – the slums, the suburbs that were blighted at birth, the formless sprawl beyond, the highways made hideous by billboards and the evidently insatiable appetite of the American motorist for fried food and the excessively enterprising notion that all abutting acreage should be devoted to satisfying it. They have assumed the corollary which is that beauty is only to be found where people are not. A number of articulate and extremely self-assured prophets – the late Theodore Roosevelt, the late Gifford Pinchot, the late Harold Ickes, the late Richard Neuberger, the late Bernard DeVoto and the happily highly extant Stewart Udall – have driven home the point in speech and print. The result has been the preservation of a great deal of wilderness that would otherwise have been lost to desecration, and everyone should be grateful.

But in fact, man at his best has done far more for landscape than this implies. The surviving English countryside, hedged, cultivated, trimmed and green, is lovely; a couple of thousand years ago the unkempt fens and forests and occasional patch of poor tillage could not have been very attractive. Similarly with France. The Rhine and Moselle would not be interesting without the vineyards, and Iowa with the red barns and green corn must be more agreeable than when it was a monotonous waste of high grass. Northern Vermont with its pastureland, barns and rich smell of cow manure is much more attractive than southern Vermont which is much closer to wilderness. Farmers, unlike outdoor advertisers and those who serve the motorist, have no apologies to make to nature.

2

The agriculture of the Scotch did less for the landscape than most. The architecture, as I have observed, was intrinsically an eyesore. So, in general, were the Scotch. The forest had been left in very untidy form. Yet, in conjunction with the seasons, there was a sufficient and changing loveliness. The fields of ten or twelve acres were a mosaic of endlessly varied design. In the spring, some showed the deep green of the winter wheat. In others, the black wet earth dried gradually to a light brown and the teams plodded over it to prepare for the spring grain and corn. Summer came with the fruit blossoms, the pastel shades of the oats and, a little later, the strong green of the corn. Then the hayfields were stripped to a greenish brown and the wheat and corn to a yellow and amber. In the autumn, the wheat fields turned green again and furrows of the fall plowing showed startlingly black against the first snow. Then the snow covered the whole land. On some days there was no color at all; only the dead gray of the driving storm.

In the common theory of farm management, farmers seek to maximize their net income. The Scotch were certainly not averse to net income but their equal concern was with minimizing gross outlay. They did not care to spend money for personal consumption if it could be avoided. And they did not care to spend it for productive purposes either if that could be prevented. To spend either their own or borrowed money meant some risk of loss. The goal of their agriculture was a safe, one-way flow of income, the flow being in their direction.

The basic farm, as I have noted, was a hundred acres. This included cropland, rough pasture and a woodlot. The basic labor force was the farmer, his wife and his sons. The first problem in eliminating outlay was to eliminate the need for hired labor.

Most of the work on a hundred-acre farm could, in fact, be performed by one man and a team of horses. A few tasks – haying, harvesting, cutting wood, breaking a colt – required two people, and a very small number of tasks, such as threshing, required a crew. Beyond a certain time the Scotch were reluctant to work their wives in the fields. But a young wife could, it was felt, give a hand on those tasks where two people were required. And as she grew older, sons became available to take her place. If a crew was required, the Scotch "changed work." The neighbors came over and helped, and this labor was repaid in kind. The annual payroll thus remained at nil.

But implicit in this economy was an arrangement of tasks which, while avoiding peaks and valleys in the need for labor, kept the one man reasonably employed the year around. This was accomplished by a combination of live-stock and field husbandry which spread the demand for labor very adequately over the year. The animals required a good deal of attention though the Canadian winter but could do very well by themselves on the summer pasture. The field crops confined their demands to the summer and these, in turn, had their own well-considered sequence. Oats, the basic cereal for livestock and on which the Scotch themselves started the day, were in the ground and growing before the corn land needed to be prepared. Beans came just before or just after the corn. Then came haying and then, in measured succession, the wheat, oat and bean harvest. Equally important were the tasks such as cutting wood, taking grain to the gristmill, putting the manure on the land (hauling shit in the brief language of the average clansman) which were undemanding as to time. These filled up the space between the jobs that could not be postponed.

A good farm manager was, perhaps most of all, a man who combined the tasks compelled by season with the more per-missive operations in an intelligent order or priority. Every once in a while there would be someone for whom the intel-lectual problem would be simply too great. He would do the wrong things first, the right things last or, in the more common case, would always be hopelessly behind on everything. His neighbors regarded him with pity and sorrow but, perhaps most of all, with secret satisfaction as a visible proof of their own personal superiority.

This timetable was, of course, terribly vulnerable to bad weather. A cold wet spring would delay spring seeding and put this into the time reserved for preparing corn or bean land. A wet June could shove haying into the wheat harvest. And so forth. The community set considerable store by equanimity in these matters, but for a certain number this was not possible. This minority watched the weather nervously and impatiently and complained bitterly when it did not accord with their needs. They invited adverse comment.

"Johnny Morrison git on the ground this morning?"

"Yeh, I saw him. Over by the culvert he could've used the *Lusitania*."

"It's a late spring."

"You got to take it as it comes."

3

The same intricate combination of crops with animal husbandry that minimized the need to pay for outside labor minimized also the need to pay for anything else. In our neighborhood, wheat and beans were sold for cash. Everything else – oats, oat straw, hay, corn and more occasionally roots and barley were fed to beef cattle, hogs, sheep and chickens. The animals turned the feed into salable products or into manure which largely eliminated the need for commercial fertilizer. The combination of crops, including the generous supplies of legumes for feed, also sustained the soil. The horses also turned their feed into energy which eliminated the need to purchase gasoline. (The Scotch came eventually to tractors but with considerable reluctance.) From the red and white grade Shorthorns (which, though kept for beef, were expected to produce milk for the household as well), the white Yorkshire or red Tamworth hogs, from the chickens of uncertain ancestry and from the orchards and gardens came the principal components of the family ration. However, the Scotch made no fetish of self-sufficiency in personal consumption. Once they had made their own cloth and ground their own wheat. But they had sensibly come to agree that factories and mills could do some things much more efficiently than they. Too much town-bought food remained a mark of profligacy. No one could think of buying canned fruit, jam or marmalade at the store. But only the most backward clans considered it a mark of merit to live completely from their land. Adam Smith was a Scot and while none of our neighbors had heard of him, his enunciation of the principle of division of labor was respected within reason.

4

On our farm the new year began not on January 1, which was a date of purely formal significance with the deepest and deadest part of the winter still to come, but in March with the arrival, as to timing, of the least permissive of all farm tasks, namely the tapping of the maples. The sun, when it shone, would now have traces of warmth. But the gray snow-banks would be still in the woods and the nights were still cold, for a run of sap must be refreshed by a nightly frost. No agricultural operation has ever been invested with so much glamour as the making of maple syrup and the reason is simple: none ever had such magic.

We tapped about two hundred trees, few enough so that we knew the personality of each. In a hollow on the south-east corner of the woods was a vast gnarled specimen which always had its three buckets full and often running over. I still think of that tree with affection, admiration and grati-tude. On the more exposed westerly side of the wood were almost equally sizable specimens which scarcely produced a drop. We regarded them with dislike and resentment. Like Massachusetts Democrats they had successfully divorced promise from performance.

Sap in those days was collected in a wooden tub mounted on a sleigh or stoneboat. A circular track wound through the black, silent woods. The horses pulled the tub from point to point along this track. At each stop we fanned out with pails to collect the sap from the red buckets. If the run was good there might be a pleasant air of urgency about this task for numerous buckets would be spilling over. The sap was then boiled in a flat rectangular pan, about three feet by six or seven, which sat on a cement arch over a vigorous log fire. Immediately back of the arch, from which the operation could be watched, and with the whole front open to the fire, was the small, shed-roofed sugar shanty. As everyone has heard but only the fortunate know at firsthand, there is no aroma on earth like that of boiling sap. In good years it was necessary to boil all night to keep abreast of the run. Then hour after hour the white steam billowed off into the black night or, on occasion, rolled into the shanty as a special reward. Neighbors who did not make syrup came across the fields and through the woods to sit and watch the fire and the steam and enjoy the smell. One could take a dipper, dip out a pint or two of the thickening sap, cool it in a snowbank and drink it all. It combined a heavenly flavor with a remarkable laxative effect.

The flavor of the syrup then produced was far better than what a less fortunate generation now gets from Vermont or Quebec. I learned the reason in what I believe was my first introduction to scientific method. Two brothers named John and Angus McNabb, who lived over near the Thames River, went into production of maple syrup on a commercial basis: they bought covered buckets and an evaporator and a galvanized tank for the sap and set out to make a quality product. It was bland and tasteless and Jim McKillop showed them why.

As the sap dripped into the open buckets, quite a few dried leaves fell in too. A large number of brown moths were also attracted by the moisture, sugar or both. So were the field mice. Jim rightly suspected that these had something to do with the flavor and on the night of the experiment, he put a quart or so of water into a sap bucket and added a handful of moths, two dead mice and several milligrams of mouse droppings which he had got from a mouse's nest. He boiled all of this into a good thick stock and added it to a gallon of the insipid McNabb syrup. There was no question; the flavor was miraculously improved.

For years in the United States the colleges of agriculture, state experiment stations, Beltsville, food processing companies, canners, container manufacturers, Birdseye people and advertising agencies have been proceeding on the assumption that nothing counts so much in food as purity. Purity, quite possibly, has its place. But there is considerable need for a research project along the lines of Jim McKillop's experiment to ascertain how much of the flavor once associated with our staple foods was the result of soundly conceived contamination.

5

The maple season or, at the latest, the time for seeding spring grains, was greatly welcomed by the farmers for another reason. It was the beginning of escape from the thralldom of chores. Livestock were out of doors and eventually on their own pasture. The whole day was free for the tight succession of tasks – preparing, seeding, planting, harvesting – which were considered the serious business of the farm. For while this system of agriculture was designed to keep a man occupied during the winter the winter work was considered tedious and a trifle degrading. As cattle, horses, poultry and to a lesser extent the sheep came into winter quarters, they required the same increase in personal services as a tourist coming from a camping trip to a hotel. These were the chores. To confess that one was "only doing chores" was to imply that one had not been really employed.

At first glance, it was rather pleasant work. One went into the half-dark barn at half past six or seven to hear the cows protesting comfortably at the ending of their night of rest and contemplation. The milking of the one cow, the release of the suckling calves to the rest, and the feeding of cattle and horses took an hour. After breakfast, another three hours was needed to throw down and prepare feed, turn the stock out for water, groom the horses, clean the stables and nail up the astonishing number of things which, in any twenty-four-hour period, would come loose.

Partly this work was disliked as all personal service is disliked. While animals are less officious than people, they are, in their own way, as quietly demanding and many can convey the same impression that the world was made for them. This naturally breeds resentment. But the more important problem lay in the brevity of the work cycle. Clearly the most unfortunate people are those who must do the same thing over and over again, every minute, or perhaps twenty to the minute. They deserve the shortest hours and the highest pay. The Scotch had no experience of this industrial drudgery but they did compare those tasks that had to be done every day with those that were related to the more spacious cycle of the seasons and thus had to be performed but once a year. They much preferred the latter.

One learned of all this from cleaning out the cow stables. It was a far from unpleasant task. One shoveled the accumulation in an unfastidious way; the metal rang against the concrete with brisk clang. Presently one could look with satisfaction at a stretch of clean and glistening concrete. But even before the fresh bedding was brought in, the enviable peristalsis of the bovine would begin to work its havoc. First from one direction then from another would come the rhythmic plopping sounds. In an hour or two one's handiwork would be in an advanced state of destruction. In contrast, one could look down a row of beans from which the grass and Canada thistle had been hoed away, and know it would remain fairly clean for the rest of the summer.

In World War I, as I have elsewhere noted, passion for the Allied cause burned very low among the Scotch. But here and there a lad joined up in advance of conscription. He then went off to serve in the armies of Field Marshal Sir Douglas Haig where, in all but the most exceptional instances, he was promptly killed. It was invariably said that he went because he was tired of doing chores.

V

The Men of Standing

At first glance, the Scotch would seem to have comprised one of the world's more egalitarian communities. While some were poor, none was rich. All worked with their hands and went as equals to the polls. No man's income was reflected in his dress or reliably in his house. The conventions of the community required that income and liquid assets be a secret between a man and his wife. In any case, farm income, unlike salary income, yields no exact figure by which people can be known and graded with precision. (Given the respect accorded to money by this culture, accurate information on the income and assets of the members would have been of considerable interest.) The common social distinction of all industrial communities, capitalist and communist alike, is between those who give (or transmit) orders and those who take them. But in this community, a

45

few hired hands apart, everyone worked for himself. The Scotch set much store by this. In the brief moments of philosophical reflection, the point was often made about farming.

"It's hard work but a man's his own boss." It did not occur to my neighbors that this might signify a hard taskmaster or, on occasion, one of questionable competence.

Yet, in fact, this was a highly stratified society. The community gave a good deal of attention to the question of precedence. There was also an agreeable certainty as to where a man stood. This last is important. If one must have a hierarchy it adds greatly to peace and security of mind if it is made clear to everyone just where he belongs.

2

There were three social classes. At the bottom were those who, although by all outward signs they were treated like everyone else, did not enjoy full citizenship. Their views did not command respect; no one would think of quoting them except possibly as an example of error. They also knew they did not belong and were reconciled to the fact in varying degree.

At the top, in turn, were the Men of Standing. They were so described and, except in rare instances, were also aware of their position. Others sought their views and in some measure accepted them, especially on matters removed from the common knowledge of the community. A measure of guidance was needed on who had burned down the Canadian Parliament buildings; it was believed that some drunken Tory had tossed his cigar into a pile of paper but the opposing

theory that it was done by the Germans needed expert
rebuttal. On the causes of the burning of the McWilliam
house everyone naturally had an opinion of his own.

Between the disenfranchised and the Men of Standing
were the much larger group whose views determined the
position of the others. The number of contented outsiders in
any society is always small. The lecturer who never got to be
professor, the newspaperman who has descended into public
relations and the politician who, however righteously, is out
of office, all nurture a deep if secret sorrow. But we also, all
too often, underestimate the capacity of men for contentment. One can be a professor without being an Oppenheimer,
a pundit but not an Alsop or a politician without being a
Kennedy. Most of the Scotch were content to be considered
ordinary citizens so long as they could determine who,
because of being better or worse, were not. This they
addressed themselves to assiduously.

More than politics, the weather, crop prospects, prices or
any other topic, the Scotch discussed one another. The
ideas, behavior and misdeeds of third persons are alluring
topics in all societies; they undoubtedly owe some of their
fascination to the omnipresent sense of indecency in talking
about someone who isn't around to defend himself. Be this
as it may, the Scotch talked constantly, clinically and
unabashedly about each other. A man's farming methods,
marketing decisions, livestock purchases, machinery acquisi-
tions, wife, family, relatives, temperament, drinking, stomach
complaints, tumors, personal expenditures, physical appearance and his political, social and economic views were dwelt
on in detail by his neighbors. Out of this discussion came
the consensus as to his place. All distinctions are, in some

degree, vicarious and thus invidious. But few could claim to be founded on so intimate an examination of person and personality. And while the Scotch did not quickly change their minds about those to whom they had accorded positions of honor or had excluded from membership, they kept their people subject to constant scrutiny. If there must be an aristocracy, it is well no doubt that it be kept under constant surveillance.

3

Some of the excluded, to begin with the lowest class, suffered their segregation for purely objective reasons. No hired man had full citizenship. A good worker might be much praised but he was still a hired man. To belong, a man had to own land and this requirement also excluded the comparatively rare family which rented land. We heard – and the *Farmer's Advocate* and other farm journals were at pains to point out – that in England and in Iowa a tenant farmer was often just as respectable as a man who owned land. The Englishmen and the Iowans were entitled to their tolerance but it was not so with us. Our neighbors made no fetish of land; none was ever seen holding the good earth in his cupped hands and gazing soulfully at the sky, and any such behavior would have been taken as indication of incipient mental disorder. But it was cheap land that had brought our ancestors from Scotland in the 1830s and '40s and anyone who didn't own some by (say) 1925 was pretty obviously a failure.

As a souvenir of Colonel Talbot's design for an unearned increment, a certain number of families still farmed fifty-acre tracts – the original inheritance. This did not qualify a man either – a man who farmed a fifty was not taken seriously on any important subject and would not ordinarily be elected to public office. Since it was perfectly possible for a hired man, tenant or a fifty-acre farmer, by combining diligence and rigid economy with a large mortgage, to own a hundred acres, these barriers to acceptance were not as harsh as they sounded. No agitator ever arose to denounce them. The people so excluded were not very competent. If it hadn't been land they would probably have lost out for some other reason.

A man was also excluded from society if he were either unneighborly or dishonest. But these faults were so rare that almost no one was ever disqualified. No one ever locked his house or feared that his livestock might be stolen. Men stuck to their bargains and negotiated their disputes. One drinking man apart, none of our neighbors had ever been inside a courtroom. The nearest police officer with jurisdiction was twenty miles away; during the twenty years that I knew the community, I never heard that he had occasion to visit it.

Men were honest because public opinion would have ruthlessly excluded from the society a man who, in the local language, "was not quite straight." The judgment would have been certain and final and the punishment would have extended to his wife and children. Only a hardened criminal who was also a case-hardened hermit could have survived such public obloquy. A man would have been excluded with almost equal severity if he had shown himself to be unneighborly. Every farm was subject to sudden emergencies. Wives or livestock had difficult births; death struck; a barn had to be raised or a horse removed from a well. There were also the regular jobs, notably threshing, which required a crew.

The common law on these matters was also clear and well enforced. A man was obliged to put his neighbor's need ahead of his own and everyone did. Occasionally there were complaints that a man called for help too readily. But no one ever declined. Again the social penalty would have been too severe. It is a great mistake to imagine that prisons and fines are the only means that a community has of enforcing its laws. Nor are they necessarily the most drastic.

4

Three other things could lead to loss of full citizenship but with somewhat less certainty than, say, the ownership of insufficient land. These were alcohol, laziness and ignorance.

The Scotch were divided into two groups, those who drank and those who didn't. If a man drank like a gentleman, it would not hurt his position in the community. Unfortunately it was not on record that anyone ever had. Men drank for only one reason, namely to get drunk. No one imagined that alcohol had any other purpose. In consequence, a drinking man regularly ended up bruised, battered and, in the absence of an especially talented horse, in the ditch. If this happened only on rare and festive occasions, it did not hurt too much. But if it occurred with any frequency – if neighbors had regularly to come in and do a man's chores while he was being restored after a tear – it cost him his membership. He lost it immediately if he got put on the Indian list.

This curiosity of sumptuary legislation enabled the wife of a habitual drinker to have her husband proclaimed an honorary aborigine. In Ontario, as in other North American jurisdictions, the sale of alcohol to the surviving tribesmen was subject to heavy penalties. These penalties applied to all on the list. Although to be on the Indian list involved total disgrace, it was not supposed that it ever stopped a determined drinker from getting liquor. There were many tales of how wives whose proscribed husbands had succeeded in getting drunk had had the hell beat out of them.

The traditions of the community required everyone to like work or say that he did. A good man did not shrink from the tasks of pure drudgery – pitching hay, pulling a crosscut saw, forking manure. But not everyone could sustain the required reputation. A few got started later in the morning than others, were tolerant of thistle and fallen fences, had to go more often to town or yielded more readily to unpleasant weather or the notion that wives were expendable. They often compounded their felony with excuses – unshod horses, lumbago, broken tools – which everyone knew to be bogus.

This did not lead to automatic exclusion. Our next-door neighbor was Bert McCallum. His house, unpainted and surrounded by tall spare spruce, was on the west of his farm; ours, sheltered by friendlier maples, was on the east side of ours so that we were only a couple of minutes apart. Bert was unquestionably lazy. His barns were in disrepair; something of importance fell off his buildings each year and was never nailed back. His agriculture involved the minimum expenditure of energy; the result in everything from weeds to drainage was deplorable. But Bert was almost everyone's best friend. He was a small man with merry eyes and a quick laugh. Though bald in principle, wispy locks of undernourished hair strayed over his head at random. His mind was well-stored with information on a large number of practical matters – how to handle an unruly horse, give it emergency aid, shingle a shed, or prescribe for piles. He always handled the stacking of the straw which was the one skilled job at a threshing. His instinct indeed was to be helpful on everyone's problems except his own. He was an authority on all of the things, interesting, amusing, ridiculous and mildly obscene, that had happened in the township in the previous twenty years. His house, such of it as remained, was a kind of informal neigh-borhood club, a place where on a winter evening anyone might drop in. Bert sat in his sock feet by the stove and made everyone welcome. Unlike many good conversationalists he seemed on occasion to enjoy listening.

Yet Bert only narrowly escaped the consequences of his indolence. It was discussed and in degree condemned. But there were always people – my father was one – who turned the conversation to Bert's virtues which everyone had to concede. So he was allowed to escape with the reputation of being a little too easy-going. But a lesser man would have been convicted and lesser men were. About a mile from our place on Willey's Sideroad near the school was an excep-tionally devout citizen who prayed and read the Scriptures every morning. His piety, which was very rare among the Scotch, was supposed to be what kept him from getting onto his fields at a decent hour. It did not earn him forgiveness, at least among the mortal. He was considered to be of no account; the bolder children, sensing that they had a duty to perform, shouted "Lazy Jim" at him on their way home from school.

The most interesting grounds for exclusion was ignorance. Most societies are reluctant so to label a man; they
would more readily call him a sex fiend or a crook. This is
because people are wary of the reputation of intellectual
arrogance. The Scotch were subject to no such fears. If a
man lacked information or the ability to put knowledge to
useful purpose, this deficiency was part of the community
consensus. In consequence, it paid him no attention and
denied him respect. He might talk but no one listened. From
an early age we knew that certain people were simply dis-
missed from consideration as ignorant.

If a man didn't make sense, the Scotch felt it was mis-
placed politeness to try to keep him from knowing it. Better
that he be aware of his reputation for this would encourage
reticence which goes well with stupidity. And there is
advantage in having the unwary and undiscriminating on
notice. The Scotch were strikingly immune to demagogy.
One reason was the total lack of hesitation in ascribing
ignorance to demagogues. Potential followers were warned
from the outset.

As a small personal footnote, I have never thought the
practice of the Scotch in this respect entirely wrong. As a
result I have rarely managed to avoid telling the intellectu-
ally obtuse what I feel they ought to know. Even when I
have remained silent, I have usually succeeded in convey-
ing an impression. It shows the influence of upbringing. It
is not a formula for personal popularity or political success
and, for a diplomat, it can complicate relations with the
State Department.

I turn now to the characteristics which distinguished the
highest class, the Men of Standing.

5

To achieve distinction in this community, one needed to have all of the normal requirements of membership in something more than merely adequate amount. A Man of Standing was likely to have more than a hundred acres, although land in large amounts did a man no good. The McMillan boys who farmed, rather badly, a large flat and poorish area near Dutton got no extra credit for their acres. A Man of Standing had, as a matter of course, to be strictly sober, a diligent worker and a competent farmer. Beyond these necessary but by no means sufficient conditions were the special factors which, depending on circumstance, assisted a man up this ladder.

Regrettably perhaps, family was one. No one would have dreamed of suggesting that one clan was inferior to another, and certainly none would have conceded it. Yet it was tacitly agreed that some were better. The McDiarmids, Fergusons, Blacks, McAlpines, McCrimmons, Elliotts and a goodly number of McKillops were of this elite. So, I am obliged to say, were the Galbraiths. We were strongly cautioned against suggesting our superiority and, as a youngster, I found this a baffling restraint. For a long while, I swung between disavowing it and apologizing for it. Neither seemed a wholly satisfactory solution.

Size was also an important crutch. The Men of Standing were usually, although not invariably, very large. In this, the Scotch were not alone; most societies favor tall men and discriminate against the short and, since this seems manifestly unfair, a conspiracy of silence covers the whole thing. The short man does show that he is aware of his disadvantage for he rarely encounters a tall man without inquiring how he finds beds that fit, what he does in a railway berth or a modern automobile, or how is the weather up there. These are passive admissions of inferiority. The tall man never dreams of replying in kind – of asking the small man how he reaches up to tie his shoelaces – for he senses that he is struggling under a handicap and is too decent to mention it. In 1944 in commenting on his forthcoming contest with Thomas E. Dewey, Franklin Roosevelt said that people would always vote for the big man with the little dog in preference to the little man with the big dog. So, of course, they did.

The superior confidence which people repose in the tall man is well merited. Being tall, he is more visible than other men and being more visible, he is much more closely watched. In consequence, his behavior is far better than that of smaller men. Along with the Galbraiths, many of the Blacks, McDiarmids and McKillops were very tall.

Animals were also used by the Scotch as a social lever and more intelligently than in most societies.

Almost instinctively people turn to animals, alive or dead, to advance their position but the strategy of doing so is poorly understood. Men and women who sense their inferiority seek to compensate by getting the support of superior horses, dogs or dead mink. They often succeed only in suggesting the contrast. Nothing so accentuates a used skin, desiccated hair, fibrous breasts, angular knees and gnarled legs as a rich and glossy fur coat. At horse shows, the crowd subconsciously compares the slope-browed and slack-chinned men who ride horses with the magnificent beasts that carry them.

However, distinguished animals add to the distinction of distinguished people. This the Scotch understood. The average clansman had average livestock and avoided sub-jecting himself to unfavorable comparisons. Those who felt able to run the risk had good livestock and were admired for their judgment. The Scotch were not especially fond of horses and they detested dairy cattle. A good herd of beef cattle – Shorthorns, Aberdeen Angus or Herefords – was the mark of a distinguished family. Good sheep and good collie dogs also added to a man's position.

6

The decisive source of esteem, the obverse of that which led to exclusion for ignorance, was information and the ability and willingness to put it to sensible use. This was, by all odds, the most admired trait. It was partly a matter of edu-cation and even those clansmen who considered education unnecessary for their own families and likely to inculcate an aversion to manual labor, deferred to it in others. But edu-cation was only important if combined with good sense. It was, if anything, a handicap if combined with a tendency to suggest silly or extravagant courses of action. The community did not suffer fools gladly. It liked educated fools least of all.

But neither was it sufficient merely to make good sense. There were quite a few men who were well informed and wise but who never got beyond a statement of their views. Only a thin line divides the articulate man of wisdom from the windbag. The Scotch expected a man to prove his wisdom by putting it to useful purpose.

And his useful wisdom could not be confined to such areas of immediate or ultimate self-interest as his own farm or church. A man needed to act on improvement of the roads, the promotion of telephone service, the cooperative purchases of binder twine, or the management of the Wallacetown Fair. He should certainly serve on the Township Council. It was also important that in all his actions he bear in mind his neighbors' concern for saving money.

The Men of Standing had, in short, to earn their esteem. This had a highly practical aspect. Every community needs a great many communal services. To pay for them is expensive; and only a poor class of talent is available for money. By rewarding such work with honor and esteem, the very best men can be had for nothing. Only a minority of the Scotch were susceptible to such blandishment. But those who were not sensed the importance of according it to those who were. Thus, it was a very good thing to be a Man of Standing and a very good thing to have them in sufficient supply.

VI

Technological Progress

O nce the Scotch must have displayed a phenomenal
capacity for innovation and adaptation in their farming
methods. The transition from the spare, wet and treeless
crofts of the Highlands and the Western Isles to the lush
forests, deep soil and strong seasons of the land by the Lake
could scarcely have been more dramatic. It is true that they
had always lived in intimate association with their cattle
and sheep; to understand these in Scotland was to understand them in Ontario. But the soils, crops, crop rotation,
the insects and plant diseases, the problems of farm architecture, machinery and drainage, even the wagon that went
to town, were all different. Within a matter of a few months,
men made the transition from an agricultural system in
which they were guided by the experience of centuries to
one where a very great deal depended on a man's capacity

to figure things out for himself or imitate with discrimination those who could.

However, by the time of which I am telling, most of the problems had been solved. Few if any of the solutions were wholly satisfactory – seed selection was poor, rust and smut exacted a toll, so did bugs, drainage was imperfect, barns were inefficient and highly combustible and even the animal husbandry in which the Scotch were imagined to be especially gifted suffered a large number of low-yielding animals which were troubled in turn by disease, pests and parasites. The Scotch were not bad farmers and some of the clansmen were a lot better than others. (Those families which went in for education, emphasizing quality rather than quantity in their offspring, were notably better than those who bred for pure labor power and forthrightly insisted that what a farmer needed was a strong back and a weak mind.) But stabilization had set in. The formula "It was good enough for my auld man so it's good enough for me" combined a decent respect for one's ancestors with economy of thought.

Working against this contentment were various official instruments of progress – agricultural fairs, the agricultural extension service, the agricultural schools and colleges. All functioned with remarkable inefficiency. The reason for this failure I have observed many times since and in places as far removed from rural Ontario as Orissa and the highlands of Peru. Those concerned with progress attribute to the farmers the goals and values which they think they should have. They design their measures accordingly. But the farmers, holding in fact quite different values, either pay no attention or turn the programs of the uplifters to wholly unexpected ends.

2

In the case of the annual exhibition of the West Elgin Agricultural Society, known colloquially as the Wallacetown Fair, the people in charge of progress rightly recognized the interest of the Scotch in making money. But they did not see that this was nearly total. Where money was involved, the Scotch were not inclined to make any of the compromises that a sporting competition required.

The Wallacetown Fair was held each year in the last days of September in the most golden of the autumn days. It was one of the few days of recreation that every clansman allowed himself and his family. On the second day of the fair, everyone was present. There was a small midway where one could win kewpie dolls by throwing rings on hooks, buy fresh sugar taffy, knock over tenpins with baseballs, and in fortunate years, ride on a merry-go-round. Sometimes an itinerant entrepreneur tried to set up with dice. A specially appointed constable closed him down. The Scotch were not only disinclined to gamble but they did not look kindly even on the opportunity. On both days of the fair, there were also harness races. It was always rumored that there was some informal wagering by an exiguous and undefined sporting element but, in the main, the races were for the purpose of ascertaining whether one horse could go faster than another.

All of this was assumed to be decorative, the sugar coating of the pill. The serious business of the fair was the improvement of husbandry. To this end, the farmers brought their cattle, sheep, hogs, fruit, roots and vegetables and their wives brought needlework, pies and cakes and other products of the domestic arts. Back of this competition lay a year of struggle. Herd sires were selected and herds improved; better seed was selected or bought; orchards were pruned and sprayed; vegetable gardens were cultivated with loving care; the womenfolk diligently practiced their needlework, fancywork, baking and other household skills. Competition is the breath of life. The agricultural authorities of the Province wisely subsidized this competition by contributing generously to the prize money. This intensified the struggle to improve.

Or so it should have been. However, the Scotch recognized quite sensibly that if everyone entered the competition, the money available to any single competitor would be negligible and the trouble would be too great. So by common consent the money was allotted to a handful of families who came to consider it their own.

Thus, we had a very good herd of purebred Shorthorns. So did Duncan Brown who lived a few miles away on the Back Street. Starting early in the morning of the second day of the fair, we and the Browns drove our best animals to Wallacetown and into the fair grounds by the back or cattle gate. It was very exciting to arrive. Other farmers would be unloading sheep and pigs; a few families who kept good horses would be cleaning harness, wiping buggies or maneuvering their highstrung trotters through the crowd. There was a rich smell of cigar smoke and horse manure. In the near distance the Muncey-Oneida Indian band, from the reservation some ten miles to the north, would be tuning up with a spine-tingling succession of squeaks and oomphs.

In the late morning or early afternoon, the judging commenced. If first prize went to the Browns, second came to us or vice versa. It all averaged out in the end. Neither we nor the Browns were in the slightest measure stimulated by the exercise. It was simply that there was no way one could so easily pick up thirty or even forty dollars in the course of one day. No ordinary husbandman would have dreamed of anything so impractical as to try improving his herd in order to compete with us. We had no need to improve to get the money. In the case of the Shorthorns, the prize money was divided. For Herefords, every cent went every year to the McNeils.

The livestock prizes did go to the better farmers of the neighborhood. For other products, the reward went, on the whole, to the more backward members of the community. In the case of mangels, turnips, squash, pumpkins, watermelon and potatoes, the prizes were comparatively small. So the wives of some of the poorer farmers took a little extra care of their gardens and got the money. By common understanding the reward belonged to them. We would not have dreamed of taking a watermelon or an apple to the fair; it would have taken money from those to whom it belonged and it would have implied, in addition, that we didn't have enough to do. The encouragement to handicrafts was equally exiguous. The same women brought the same patchwork quilts and embroidery to the fair every year and would have been indignant if some parvenu had to come in with something new of competitive quality.

However, the adverse effect of the fair in subsidizing unproductive activities could easily be exaggerated.

3

The other instruments of progress – the extension service, the Ontario Agricultural College and the various services of the Ontario Department of Agriculture – assumed that the Scotch wanted to make as much money as possible. As a result, they fell afoul of the desire to save money. They had other failings as well.

The physical manifestation of these services in our community was the Agricultural Representative, the Ontario equivalent of the county agent. He was in those days a fat, totally bald and very good natured man called Charley Buchanan. Charley was a bachelor, a good mixer, a nearly incoherent speaker, and, within limits, a believer in progress. For a time he got around the muddy roads on a motorcycle. Then the Provincial authorities bought him a car. He worked faithfully. Most of the Scotch had nothing whatever to do with him.

This was partly because he was based in a small office in Dutton and did not operate a farm himself. Below a certain level of income and sophistication, practicing cultivators always suspect advice from those who do not farm themselves. This is not, as commonly supposed, because they attach some mystical importance to toil. (This belief often leads advisers to seek the confidence of farmers by showing that they are not afraid to wield a fork or shovel.) It is because the farmers rightly sense that there is danger in the counsel of any man who does not himself have to live by the results. As agricultural services have developed and spread around the world, millions of farmers have benefited from the recommendations and advice. But, a less celebrated fact, quite a few thousands, at one time or another, have received a bum steer. They and not their advisers have paid the price. They may have gone hungry, lost a child or their livestock, or their land. What is often deplored as the con-servatism of farmers or peasants is, in fact, the healthy respect of men with a small margin for error for what is fully proven within range of their own eyesight.

But the greater difficulty was that everything Charley advised cost money. Some of this was simply ill-considered. The experts at the Ontario Agricultural College (which I later attended) had expensive designs for barns which afforded a maximum of contentment to the cows but which, as the farmers quickly saw, would add little to their income. Poultry houses similarly became palaces. The experts shuddered at the thought of an unpedigreed bull. Once we obtained some plans for draining a rather marshy tract that we had acquired up Hogg Street from the home farm. It was a marvel of hydrologic excellence and would have cost considerably more than the farm was worth. The experts regularly priced themselves out of our market.

But even where Charley's recommendations involved some consideration of cost and returns – an outlay for fertil-izer justified by the value of the prospective increase in the crop – the Scotch were not easily persuaded. Spending money even when it might mean more money was painful. And perhaps also unwise. For with the increased prospect of gain came the increased possibility of loss. Fertilized crops can be lost in a drought and then the money for the fertil-izer is lost along with all else. Better try for less and be safe. Charley was a man of good sense and recognized that his recommendations were usually unwelcome and refrained from pressing them. My father, who believed in principle in progress and, I think, sensed Charley's problem, used to consult him meticulously on sprays for our fruit trees. By quietly cutting the recommended sprays from three or four to one, he found he could follow his advice on this matter without undue expense. For the rest, he also avoided any guidance by Charley.

4

Yet the agriculture of the community was not static. Each year there were a few clansmen who tried something new. They saw a chance to make money in beans; or they grew cucumbers for a new pickle factory at West Lorne; or they bought a tractor; or they built a silo; or they tried out a high-yielding variety of oats or barley. If these things worked, they were copied. If, as often happened especially with new money-making crops, they failed, the community treated the experiments with the contempt they so richly merited.

It is possible, to be quite fair, that back of some of these ideas lay the official engines of progress, including even Charley. But it is important not to exaggerate their role. The colleges of agriculture, experiment stations and extension services of the advanced farming regions of the United States and Canada have worked one of the great technical revolutions of all time. They did so because they were perfectly attuned to the farmers they served. The farmers wanted to make money and were willing to spend money to do so. The experts (tamed by the economists since the days

of which I speak and forced to prove that their recommendations would pay out) have been an admirable buttress to
this pecuniary urge. But it has been assumed that what has
worked so well with us must have an equally marvelous
effect on the agriculture of Asia, Africa, or South America.
American professional agriculturists are among the world's
greatest evangelists. In consequence, for nearly two decades,
we have been exporting our system of agricultural services to
the peasants and cultivators of the world. The results have,
on the whole, been disappointing.

This does not mean that the effort should be abandoned.
It does mean that it must be adapted to the values of those
involved. If farmers subordinate income to security of
income, this must be accepted. The desire to avoid experiments which, should they turn out badly, might preclude
eating for a year, may not be wholly foolish. And the goal of
these services is not, in the first instance, farmers as a whole.
Rather, it is that minuscule minority who can be persuaded
to accept the risks (and possibly the obloquy) of innovation
and from whom others will learn.

VII

The Polity of the Scotch

An important requirement of political democracy is that people enjoy the business of governing themselves. Parliamentary government has worked well in India and military government encountered stout objections in Pakistan because in both countries, as a legacy of British rule, the rituals of parliamentary government – elections, by-elections, parliamentary decorum, the question hour, speeches, heckling – are regarded with great affection. A dictatorship provides no comparable distractions. One test of how well democracy is regarded is the number of elections that are held. The City and Canton of Geneva has elections almost every other Sunday. In Boston, the somewhat battered cradle of American democracy, the election posters are never taken down. The Foleys and Francis X. Kellys of one contest run on the signs of those who won or lost the

last time. Other American communities are not far behind. At the other extreme, Germans who regard government as a career, Frenchmen who regard it as a somewhat dubious profession, and Italians who look upon it, on the whole, as an unpleasant necessity have far fewer elections and enjoy them much less.

Rural Ontario, by these tests, had a fairly high score. Once a year on New Year's Day, local school sections selected their school trustees, and there was an election for the township council. (A warden and county council were selected indirectly at the same time for they consisted of the reeves and deputy reeves of the various townships and municipalities comprising the county.) On the average, once every three to four years there was an election for the Dominion House of Commons, and at roughly similar intervals also for the Ontario Legislature. In addition, there were occasional plebiscites. (These in my youth were confined exclusively to the question of whether the Province of Ontario should continue to have prohibition. The cities were opposed; so were the distillers and brewers. But the rural Scotch – even and perhaps especially the drinking Scotch – were strongly in favor and their vote was always decisive. Eventually the provincial legislature had to repeal the law against the votes although possibly not the will of the majority.) In Canada, as in the United States, an election is always just over or immediately in prospect.

The Scotch took elections seriously. Local elective offices were given, as a matter of course, to the Men of Standing. They were not the only ones who sought election; from time to time some individual who was badly informed as to his rank ran for office with disastrous results. One such was a neighbor of ours, Hugh McPhail. Hughy, as he was called, was by then in his fifties and farmed adequately a hundred or perhaps a hundred and fifty acres. He was known to have some money by inheritance. He lived in a large, square red brick house with his very small wife, two young sons, and two very large unmarried sisters. While somewhat under the control of his sisters, he was able, with their help, to dominate his wife. Hughy was ambitious, energetic and did not hesitate to voice his opinions. The McPhails were a fairly prestigious clan. Unfortunately, Hughy had the reputation for being ignorant. Such were his other qualifications that he was not excluded from membership. But he was not a Man of Standing. In 1922 or thereabouts he stood for township counsellor. He campaigned hard and nearly everyone voted against him. Mostly the choice was between Men of Standing and the results were then a good deal closer.

The County of Elgin, for some forty years, was run by Mr. Angus McCrimmon, who was Crown Attorney, Mr. Kenneth McKay (for whom I was named), who was county clerk, my father, who was county auditor, and (for much of that time) the county treasurer, whose name was Benjamin Graham. All were Men of Standing.

In federal and provincial elections most of the Scotch voted as they went to church as a recurrent act of obeisance to the faith of their fathers and grandparents. (Of this more in a moment.) For a few of the clansmen elections had elements of a sporting competition. Far more of the pleasure of democratic politics is in such competition than is commonly conceded. A candidate matches his wits and lung power and his talent for persuasion and insult against the opposition in a richly rewarding contest that places no awkward premium on physical condition. And, unlike a fist fight or even ice hockey, belligerence is justified in the high name of public service, constitutional government and effective democracy.

Voters are capable of similar enjoyment. It is the instinct to competition that causes the most evocative cries of an election campaign, the shouts of "Pour it on!" and "Give 'em hell, Harry!" Quite a few of the clansmen backed the Liberals (also called the Grits and Reformers) because they wanted the competitive reward of winning and even more because they wanted the unadulterated joy of seeing the Tories lose. They imagined or at least hoped that the Tories suffered terribly in defeat.

Locally there was no real competition – there were too many Liberals – but one could always try to improve on the majority of past years. But as on other matters appurtenant to this culture, an interest in elections was sustained by their relation to the matter of making and keeping money.

2

When the Scotch settled by the Lake in the early nineteenth century in what was then called Upper Canada, they found the political life of the colony a comfortable monopoly of the privileged. At the apex was the Lieutenant-Governor, an appointee of the Crown, and almost invariably a retired general (or sometimes lesser officer) of Wellington's armies. Surrounding him and advising him were Anglican bishops, businessmen and minor members of the aristocracy who had "come out" from England to make good and were starting in at the top. There have been, one imagines, more wicked oligarchies than the Family Compact, as it was called. But, undeniably, it ruled in its own behalf. Its members took all the posts of privilege and profit under the Crown. Trade favored its merchants. Most important, land grants went to its members, or to the Church as the real estate holding company for the Compact, or to those who were in a position to pay the people who granted the land. One of the rewards of an utterly secure social position has always been the ability to take bribes from lesser folk without loss of dignity or sense of demeanment. The Scotch ranged themselves in political opposition to the Family Compact. Those by the Lake needed very little education on the subject for they had been forced to obtain the land from one of its more prominent members, the eccentric, profane and bibulous Colonel Talbot.

On one feature of democratic politics, there is something akin to a conspiracy of silence. This is the fact that in all successful democracies, the vast majority of people, including those who speak with the greatest passion, get their political affiliations not by ratiocination but by inheritance. To know how people will vote, you have only to know how their grandparents voted in the male line. Nor is it certain that any other system is tolerable. The most disturbing passages in Thucydides are those in which he tells how the Athenians (or the Corcyrans or others) were swayed *en masse* by their orators. To this open-mindedness could be attributed their worst disasters. Democracy evidently needs the stabilizing influence of a very large number of people whose voting habits are wholly predictable – who cannot be persuaded to abolish the welfare state, dismember trade unions, release the rich from taxes, or seek nuclear annihilation in accordance with the urging of some especially talented spellbinder.

In the manner of the landed South after Lincoln or the rich after Roosevelt, most of the Scotch simply kept on voting against the Family Compact and handed the habit on to their children. These were the predictable mass, the solid rank and file of the Liberal Party. However, in the latter part of the last century and the early decades of this, the tariff also became an issue of interest to the Scotch.

The Tories (later and more elegantly the Conservatives and still later and with some element of internal contradiction, the Liberal-Conservatives and then the Progressive-Conservatives) who had inherited the traditions of the Family Compact were for protection. This would build up internal Canadian commerce and manufacturing in which the members had a solid stake. It also prevented excessive dependence on markets in the United States with the possibility that the flag might follow trade to the point of political absorption. The Scotch, for their part, looked at the burgeoning markets in Detroit and Buffalo, both bigger and closer than the major Canadian centers of population, and yearned for the chance to run the risk. The Liberal Party, initially with some vigor and later with notable caution, played to their hopes. It also promised lower import tariffs on farm machinery, though less to make American machines cheaper than for its salutary effect on the great Canadian farm implement firm of Massey-Harris. The tariff issue meant that the Scotch could continue to find plausible economic reasons for voting for the Liberals, and it would have occurred to none that there were any other issues of enduring political importance.

3

Tradition and the hope for lower tariffs guaranteed the voting behavior of the overwhelming majority of the Scotch. The rest were open to some form of persuasion. On the other side, a great minority in the rural areas, were families of English or American Tory (i.e., Loyalist) descent who had never been at odds with the Compact. They were still called Tories. If passionate in their faith or if being described by a man of passion they were called rotten Tories. Even between elections, they stood a little apart.

Political effort centered naturally on the politically mobile minority among the Scotch plus the odd conservative who was considered detachable. What in many communities would be considered conventional appeals to the voter – the promise of public works or patronage – were unimportant to the extent that they were not negative in their voter appeal. Public works, especially if they seemed to be for the purpose of attracting votes, advertised their own profligacy. The Scotch used the works but condemned the profligates. In 1919, in momentary anger with both of the old parties, the farmers of Ontario organized a new party and to the surprise of themselves and almost everyone else, won a provincial election. The new government of the United Farmers of Ontario launched an ambitious highway-building program which did much to rescue rural highway users from mud as glutinous as any on earth. Previously the money had gone for canals and harbors where it couldn't be seen. The heavy expenditure on highways was highly visible. It was one of the reasons the government was thrown out when it again appealed to the country.

My father, for around half a century, was the leading Liberal of the community. He considered patronage even more damaging than public works. The better class of clansman stuck to his farm; he could not be seduced by a job on the roads or running a post office. As a result, government jobs went to the laziest and most feckless members of the community. These, in turn, became for the voters the exemplars of the government and party. Angus Graham's dubious hours and lax workmanship on his section of the highway were taken as an indication of similar standards of administration elsewhere. If the Government favored men like Angus in Dunwich, it presumably employed them in Toronto or Ottawa as well. To have to explain this away was a heavy price to pay for Angus' vote which one had anyway. The position was always much stronger when patronage was in the hands of the Conservatives.

Persuasion played a certain role with the uncommitted minority. The independent in politics is rarely in doubt as to how he will vote. But he wants the rewards of his independence, and this consists in being sought after by important people. My father kept a careful list of all who considered themselves independent with a note as to the political station of the person required as a persuader. Sometimes it would be my father; on occasion, only a call from the Member or candidate would suffice. By a poor arrangement of things, those whom the loyal party man most resented thus got the most attention.

Alas, also, my father's book contained a notation on those whose votes could only be had for money, together with the amount required. My father did not like using money in elections; he once told me that he had never bought votes until he had some feeling that the other side might be doing so or contemplating it. He also argued that only men of exceptionally inferior character sold their votes. Better have such people vote in response to a straightforward commercial transaction than in accordance with their own political convictions which were so patently nil. I confess that I have always thought that penalties for electoral fraud should run at least equally against sellers.

4

Among those who had to be bribed, there was the special case of those who sold out to both sides and then voted according to the dictates of their own highly defective conscience. One such was the aforementioned Swampy Dan Graham who lived two streets over from ours. (Poor farms but never good ones were the inspiration for a nickname.) Special precautions had to be taken to supervise Swampy Dan's voting. Balloting always took place in the Willey's Corners School which was recessed for the event. One corner of the single room was curtained off so that the ballot might be marked in privacy. The curtain also enclosed a window to provide light. Swampy Dan was required to hold his marked ballot up to the window. There it was checked by Bill Gow who, as Swampy Dan went into the booth, went out to the pump in the yard to get a drink of water. Not even the Tories questioned these precautions. The Australian ballot was not meant to protect people of such poor character as Swampy Dan.

My own introduction to politics occurred in these days. My father was a prodigious orator and from the age of six or eight, I began accompanying him to meetings. It was of some educational value, and I learned, among other things, the uses of humor. Once at an auction sale, my father mounted a large manure pile to speak to the assembled crowd. He apologized with ill-concealed sincerity for speaking from the Tory platform. The effect on this agrarian audience was electric. Afterward, I congratulated him on the brilliance of the sally by which I too had been deeply impressed. He said, "It was good but it didn't change any votes."

In 1952 and 1956, the speeches of Adlai Stevenson were spiced by similar if somewhat more elevated sallies. The best he wrote himself. Quite a number were by Arthur Schlesinger. Some were mine. Often, with appropriate circumspection, other members of the campaign party would congratulate me on some particularly pointed thrust including ones with which I had nothing to do. I always found myself recalling the earlier warning. Humor is richly rewarding to the person who employs it. It has some value in gaining and holding attention. But it has no persuasive value at all.

VIII

Education

D r. Johnson on his Scottish tour thoughtfully scruti-nized the bookshelves of his hosts for signs if not of culture at least of usefully employed literacy. He was pleas-antly surprised. The clansmen had more and better books than he expected.

Our neighbors would have accorded more closely with his expectations. Those who did not belong did not read. The community did not consider them capable of educating either themselves or anyone else and they accepted the judgment. Despite much talk about learning for its own sake an important byproduct, even in the most distinguished educational centers, is the desire to inform and impress others. The excluded had, of course, no audience.

The average clansman did not read much either. He sub-scribed to the weekly Dutton *Advance* and usually to a daily paper. But he read these journals in a cursory way after dinner or supper and purely in pursuit of fact. From *The Advance* he learned who had been born, who had married and who was dead and most of all, since this was the prime recreation of the Scotch, who had visited whom. In course of time he would have learned all of these things from his neighbors or his wife but everyone enjoys seeing the names of people he knows in print. For a brief moment you are in the company of those who are famous, notorious or both. From the St. Thomas, London (Ontario), or Toronto paper he got the weather forecast, the livestock quotations, word of any railroad or other accident, the progress of the forest fires in northern Ontario and the drought in Saskatchewan, and, between 1914 and 1918, intelligence on the unbroken string of brilliant military successes which were reported as attending Allied operations on the Western Front without, however, altering the location of the front.

He did not read books at all. If asked why he would have replied, with better reason than most, that he did not have the time. (There are few things that people who write find so distressing as the air of sympathetic but righteous superiority with which people tell you that *they* have no time to read books. By this they also imply that they have more useful employment than those who write books. Some years ago, more for reasons of commercial acquisitiveness than popular education, my publisher arranged to have me interviewed by Mr. Mike Wallace about a book I had just written. Not unnaturally Mr. Wallace did not have the time; his questions, I learned, would be put into the interview *ex post*. But it turned out that his assistant was also a busy person. She began by telling me with some energy that she did not have time to read either. Then she took me severely to task for what I had written.) The average clansman got his views not from newspapers, magazines or books but from the Men of Standing.

But the Men of Standing, with exceptions, did not read much either. They did, however, keep a close watch on the one unfailing guide to the sound position on all issues which was the Toronto *Globe*. Not even the Boston *Transcript*, which in its generally austere aspect it somewhat resembled, ever had such a committed clientele. The Scotch did not cite the views of *The Globe* with approval; they merely cited them.

All Canadian historians refer to *The Globe* as the bible of the Scotch; the *Encyclopaedia Britannica* credits it with a "tyrannical" hold on their minds. This is much too strong. It was the genius of *The Globe* that it told the Scotch what they wanted to believe and then urged them to believe it. It was strongly for the Liberal Party in which its Edinburgh-born founder, George Brown, was a dominant figure. It was suspicious of wealth, influence and social position; it stood for small enterprise, independent farmers, low tariffs and the Manchester School. In Brown's time it advocated commercial union with the United States. It defended the Sabbath and opposed alcohol. It was for public ownership of utilities and was the protector of the Ontario Hydroelectric Power Commission. It was very suspicious of trade unions, an attitude which was thought to have been heightened in 1872 by a bitter struggle between Brown and the International Typographical Union which, newly arrived from the United States, was demanding a nine-hour day. Farmers who worked from sun to sun naturally shared Brown's contempt for such sanctified malingering.

The ambition of most newspapermen is to have a strong and influential editorial policy. While it is rarely put so crassly, that presumably is to avoid errors inherent in allow-ing people to think for themselves. *The Globe*, for better or worse, succeeded more than most. In the natural course of events it merged with the Toronto *Mail & Empire*, which was the arch-exponent of King and Empire, Church, pecu-niary privilege, social position and the Tories.

Back of this somewhat restricted interest in literature lay the elementary school system to which I now turn.

2

As I have noted, the farm of Bert McCallum marched with ours on the east. On the west was a fifty-acre stretch of pasture, once a farm, which we occasionally used on a rental arrangement. On the far side of the fifty, running at right angles to Hogg Street and intersecting it was Willey's Sideroad. Seven-eighths of a mile south toward the Lake, the Sideroad crossed Clay Street at Willey's Corners, and on the southeast corner in a small lot cut out of the woods stood S.S. (for School Section) Number 4 of Dunwich Township, commonly called Willey's Corners or Willey's School. All of these monuments immortalized one Moses Willey, in my time long withdrawn from the world, from whose woods the modest real estate requirements of the school had been carved.

The school building was a plain rectangular structure of white brick and consisted of one small room together with a very small entry where we hung our coats on hooks and stowed our lunch boxes on a shelf above. At the back of the room was a large wood stove surrounded by a galvanized iron jacket. The stovepipe emerged from the stove, and just below the ceiling, it turned from the vertical to the horizontal and traversed the length of the room to disappear into the chimney at the far end. In the winter, one of the larger boys went early to the school and lit the fire, and it was his responsibility to stoke it during the day. For this duty, he was paid twenty-five cents a week and was considered, in consequence, one of the more affluent members of the community. On cold days, one was always considerably warmer on the side nearest the stove than on the other but the arrangement was by no means intolerable.

Back from the school ran a high board fence which divided the school yard into two unequal parts. The smaller part was reserved to the girls; the other was for male and general use. At the end of the fence adjacent to the woods, one in the girls' yard and one in the boys', were two privies painted red. The cordwood for the stove was stacked along the fence on the boys' side. That yard also contained a well and iron pump.

The yard was very rough and it sloped steeply from the school building to Clay Street. Thus, there was no chance that it could be used for baseball, football, basketball, volleyball or any other group games. Few things, by commonly advocated standards, are so bad for the youngster of impressionable age as team sports. Instead of causing him to think first of his own self-interest, they turn his mind to the problem of the group. He ceases to be an individualist and becomes a mere cog in a social machine.

We were safe. Our only form of organized athletics consisted of standing on the woodpile looking over the fence and down on the girls' yard and seeing how long, with the aid of snowballs, we could deny access to the girls' toilet. This surely did us no damage. It was also an interesting study of the way in which different girls reacted to alternative forms of discomfort. Those who faced the barrage promptly and with comparative calm were much admired.

3

While being protected from organized athletics, we were provided with unlimited access to the surrounding forest, and this was total joy. When we went back to school in September, the leaves would already be turning; soon the schoolyard was enclosed by a towering bank of crimson, scarlet and yellow. Sometimes it seemed to take the sunlight itself and turn it back in colors too wonderful to behold. Then the leaves fell away and so did the horizon; one could now see into the depths of the wood and on one side of the school to the meadows beyond. In the winter, all color went out of this landscape. The trees were black; the sky gray; the snow a somber white. Nothing stirred and it was a trifle fearsome. One can only imagine that winter in the Canadian woods will last forever.

But then the sun began to cut rivulets under the ice, and the snowbanks retreated to the middle of the woods. At noon, we made our way to the tidy sugar shanty, a half mile or so down in the woods, where Harry and Archie Blue made maple syrup. The maple buds became red and then a pale green, and a little knoll back of the school was covered with hepaticas, and the fence corners were filled with blue and white violets. There were also jack-in-the-pulpits and forget-me-nots and wild leeks which were delicious and left everyone with a hideous breath.

To the south of the school a few hundred yards distant was an abandoned gravel pit, and before classes were suspended for the summer, the groundhogs would come out of their burrows to sit in the sun. By sneaking up behind them, one could put a coat or sweater behind them in the hole, and taking alarm, they would dash wildly into its folds. When disentangled, they made an excellent exhibit. Few things are so fundamental as the desire of man to match his wits against those of the other mammals and fish. So insecure is he in his advantage that he regularly embalms the evidence of his victories. Once not long ago, I visited Bikaner, the capital of one of the major Rajput principalities in the deserts of western India. The large modern palace was packed to capacity with the stuffed carcasses of tigers, lions, bear, deer, zebra, giraffes and every other wild mammal of any size and distinction. They were catalogued by the year in which they had been shot. I asked if the animal rather than the Maharajah had ever won. I was assured that the family had been consistently triumphant.

4

Between twelve and fifteen children attended Willey's School in my time – roughly the years of the First World War and following. This was a small yield from the thirty or forty families entitled to the services of this academy and reflected the infertility and prudence of the Scotch. One progressed through five grades after the first, each divided into a junior and senior section. Thus, there was Primer, Junior First, Senior First, on up to Senior Fourth. Each stage was assumed to require a year. However, because of the very small number of children, there were usually only one or two in a class. The teacher often found it economical to add the children in one class to those in the next, and the consequence was a greatly accelerated rate of movement. As the result of a series of breathtaking promotions, the result less of academic merit than of academic convenience, I passed through Willey's School in five years and started high school at the age of ten.

Progress was also facilitated by the curriculum which was free from frills. We were taught reading, penmanship, arithmetic, spelling, and, in a manner of speaking, the geography and history of Canada. The Toronto authorities, who had always thought the rural Scotch in need of considerable improvement, had hopes for two other areas of instruction, namely hygiene and patriotism. The hygiene book made the not uncommon error of allowing one or two utterly impractical edicts to discredit much good sound common sense. It prescribed a nightly bath which everyone knew was silly. The teacher did not have one and neither the McFarlanes nor (when the McFarlanes moved to the larger farm) the Robbs, where she boarded, would have tolerated for a week a woman who required a washtub full of warm water before retiring. Nor could she have bathed with becoming decency in the kitchen which was the one warm room. The position on bathing being silly, we naturally suspected the advice on brushing teeth, changing wet socks and keeping away from people with colds. Credibility also suffered from the very last lesson in the book which, in an almost imperceptible concession to sex education, said we should pick out as a partner in life a healthy person of good character whom we loved. No mention was made of property which we all knew to be very important.

Patriotism was inculcated by a rendering of "God Save the King" at the beginning of each day as well as "The Maple Leaf Forever." (The more or less official anthem was "O Canada" but at this time there was still grave uncertainty as to the words.) And from time to time we had talks on the virtue and beneficence of the Royal Family to which the Scotch were rightly thought to be very indifferent. Much of this latter instruction was undertaken by the school inspector, Mr. Taylor, who visited us twice a year. A staunch imperialist, it was his view that the Prince of Wales was a particularly compelling figure for Canadian youth. We were counseled to admire and love this good and engaging young man and to make him our model in all matters of behavior and deportment. Many years later, at a party in New York, I told the Prince, who in the interim had been King and for many decades the Duke of Windsor, of this advice. He seemed relieved when he learned, on further inquiry, that I had not followed it in all particulars.

5

The Willey's School was supported financially from the local tax rates with some help from the Province and its administration was vested in three trustees, one of whom was elected each year for a term of three years by the ratepayers of the school district. The election was held town-meeting fashion at the school on a day between Christmas and New Year's. The participants walked in groups through the snow to the school and squeezed their overalled bulk into the seats meant for children. It was a recurrent trouble to the teacher that when we reassembled on the Monday following there would be black tobacco-juice stains on the floors, some with a little rivulet spreading out from what had been the source, and there would be other spots on the stove where well-sluiced shots had sizzled and fried into silence. The older boys would cite this example against her when they felt their dignity required them to have a chew, as it often did.

The election itself was a trifle cut and dried. For a few days before, there would be conversation as to who would be a good man. There were certain minimum moral qualifications. Roy Smith (a synthetic name, for his children still survive), who was of non-Scottish origin and who had served in World War I and returned with an exceptionally erotic account of his adventures in France, would not have been considered qualified. The stories had been heard with interest but they suggested that he shouldn't have much to do with children. And one had to have full membership in the community. No hired man or tenant farmer and no one who farmed fifty acres or was classed as ignorant would be considered eligible.

Two educational philosophies contended, although on the whole peacefully, for control of the school. The struggle was not, as in so many modern communities, between those

with property and those with children. In S.S. No. 4, everyone owned property. And the school trustees were almost
always elected from among parents with children in school.
Rather, the conflict was between those who believed that
education had independent utility for improving a man's
position in the community or preparing him for a profession
and those who viewed it as a necessary but burdensome and
even somewhat dangerous supplement to a strong back.

Apart from the occasional case of a frail or studious
boy who might be marked for the Presbyterian ministry,
those who viewed education in minimal terms kept their
older boys at home in the autumn until the field work was
finished. And they withdrew them from school when work
became heavy in the spring. Since it did little for them,
they wished to have the school run at minimum expense.
They resisted increases in the teacher's salary and did not
hesitate to point out that she worked only from nine to four,
had Saturdays and Sundays off and enjoyed generous holidays
in a community where holidays were almost unknown. They
opposed improvements to the school, especially those that
added to the convenience or comfort of the children. These
they felt contributed to the debilitating effects of education.

Those who attached original value to education were
anxious, by contrast, to have a well-paid teacher. And they
tended to look with favor on improvements, even those such
as better heating, which added to the comfort of the children.

As always, the issue was compromised. The $500 to $600
annual salary of those days struck a balance between the two
extremes. When the educationally inclined were dominant,
fifty or seventy-five dollars would be spent for school desks or

a better blackboard. These would tide over leaner years when the forces of economy were in power.

The conflict was also eased by the ambiguous role of the teacher. For she came to the community not only as an educator but also as a prime matrimonial prospect. Although the courting of a teacher had to be exceptionally antiseptic even by our austere standards, a minimally attractive girl could hope to find a solvent husband in a matter of two or three years. (If she didn't she moved on.) And even the young men who had been reared to regard education only as a convenience were often attracted by the idea of an educated wife. They were in favor, accordingly, of attracting a good class of girl into the community.

6

Whether S.S. No. 4 was a good school or not depends on what was expected of it. It existed, which was important, and this was because it was created and largely paid for by the people who used it. In many parts of the world, education being rightly deemed urgent, it has been decided that the central (or at a minimum a state) government should supply it. What more vital task is there? What function could have a higher claim on the resources of the larger community?

But these resources are never adequate. And even though education is important, other claims, including those of larceny, supervene. Perhaps the promise has its principal consequence in keeping the local community from providing for itself, for the promise remains though it is never redeemed.

There should be no doubt about it, the United States and Canada got school systems soon and quickly because they put the task of providing them on those who used them. Only later did those interested in education take up the task, by no means an unimportant one, of extracting supplementary support from the more remote units of government.

For those who regarded education as an unfortunate necessity, S.S. No. 4 probably provided most of the essentials. One summer Sunday afternoon sometime after I left the school, I was lying on a hammock made of fence wire and wooden slats which hung beside our house, reading *Lorna Doone*. A contemporary, a member of one of the families who held to the minimal view of education, came along and asked me what the book was about. I handed it to him and discovered he could read only by sounding out the separate syllables. His deprivation struck me as appalling, and I had the poor taste to let him sense it. He observed, blithely, that even though he were able to read well, he still wouldn't.

For anyone who might have been encouraged to read or in whom some other spark might have been aroused, or for anyone who was using S.S. No. 4 as a preparation for something more, it was unquestionably a disaster. Once we had a good teacher. Her name was Ella Belle McFarlane and she inspired everyone with something of her enthusiasm for what one could know. But she was an accident. All the rest were half-educated young females diligently but incompetently filling in the few years between puberty and the best available marriage. What we needed was a school, doubtless one that combined several smaller ones, presided over by a schoolmaster who was an experienced and educated man who would be a schoolmaster all his life and who, as in a French village, would be, so far as this depended on position rather than person, one of the senior members of the community. What we had was an improvisation. And as in much of the United States, what had once been an ingenious improvisation was by way of being considered part of the natural order of things. As the little red schoolhouse, it was acquiring a certain sanctity. A move during my youth to consolidate school districts was firmly resisted by all right-thinking people as radical.

Herein lies a danger against which we should be warned. That is premature canonization. In the annals of American diplomacy the discovery that while we might not have a foreign policy we did have airplanes seemed initially a matter of considerable note. It was natural that, in the first blush of novelty, we should name the new landing field at Washington for the inventor. But in the more mature light of history Mr. John Foster Dulles was a disastrous Secretary of State. The airfield does not even do him a service for it serves only to remind the thoughtful traveler who it was in the field of diplomacy that first substituted mobility for thought.

The tiny school on the corner served well for its moment. But it was the mark of progress not to embalm it but to replace it, along with its unlearned ladies, at the earliest possible moment.

IX

Godfearing but Unfrightened

I f one continues another seven-eighths of a mile along Willey's Sideroad past the school, one comes to the Back Street, sometimes called the Talbot Road and now Queen's Highway Number 3. When life was oriented to the Lake, this road lay along the edge of the wilderness and hence the primary name.

West on the Back Street three miles, through the lands of the McWilliams, Grahams, McColls and more McCallums and McKillops, lay the Canterbury of our community, the village of Wallacetown. Here the settlers built their churches and when, later on, the railroad had nurtured the much larger village of Dutton two and a half miles to the north, they remained faithful to their ancient associations. The Dutton churches had a metropolitan atmosphere in which the Scotch did not feel at home, although, by the standards of the world at large, Dutton was not a great metropolis – only some eight or nine hundred souls in all.

Wallacetown had a very small Catholic church, a somewhat larger Methodist congregation, a somewhat remarkable Baptist congregation whose church was situated a little distance from town, and a very large body of Presbyterians. The latter gathered for worship in a big red brick edifice on the Currie Road just north of town after giving their horses the protection of the long horse sheds in the rear.

The Presbyterians had Sunday school, morning services which were attended by the entire family, evening services from which the elders were excused and at which religion was somewhat subordinate to the preliminary rituals of mating, a weekly choir practice and a Wednesday night prayer meeting which, however, was patronized only by the exceptionally pessimistic. The Presbyterians were, in other words, a full scale religious enterprise, and their affairs were of interest even to those who did not belong. We did not belong but we knew that one of the McFarlanes passed the plate as a cover for personal economy. He did not take anything but neither did he ever put anything in. We shared with the Presbyterians an interest in whether God frowned on Angus McWilliam who copiously spat tobacco down the furnace register during his devotions. Everyone was deeply involved when the Presbyterians were riven by the Great Schism, an event to which I will return.

2

All of the Scotch believed in God. But for most this was less the result of piety than of tradition and prudence. By quite a few, prudence was not deemed to require regular church attendance, and others had found in the Covenanted Baptist Church of Canada a very satisfactory compromise between cost and convenience and caution.

This congregation, known to the community as the Old School or Hardshell Baptists, met in a plain rectangular red brick structure about a mile east of Wallacetown on the Back Street. It stood on a little hill with a small burial ground on one side and the usual horse sheds behind. This was the church we attended.

How this creed got into rural Canada I do not know. It had vague ties with similar congregations in the border states, and, on important occasions, preachers came from West Virginia and Tennessee. But there was no doubt as to its hold on the affections of the rural Scotch or the reasons. It was completely accommodated to their culture.

This became evident the moment one stepped inside the church. For it contained nothing, literally nothing, but square oaken pews and a plain wooden pulpit. Church doctrine forbade a choir, organ – in fact music of any kind. The singing of Psalms was allowed and, as accomplished by the Scotch without accompaniment of any kind, involved no violation of this ordinance. The collection of money in church was also strictly forbidden. This was not to protect the worshipers from some momentary impulse to generosity. Nor was it felt that, deep as might be the respect for God, it was unwise to subject Him to unnecessary competition.

Money was the weekday faith. To keep it out of church was to show that Sunday was sacred to a different deity.

Nor was much money needed. Central to the creed of the church was an uncompromising predestinarianism. A man was born saved or he was born damned; it was incredible that an omnipotent God could be without an advance view of the fate of Malcolm "Little Malc" Graham or even that of the Honourable John C. Elliott, M.P., Postmaster General of the Dominion of Canada and by some margin the most distinguished member of the congregation. Accordingly pleas, persuasion and warnings were redundant; they could not alter the outcome. It followed, further, that money spent for an eloquent pastor was wasted; a competent exposition of man's inevitable fate was all that was required. It was a still further tenet of the faith that a good preacher was inspired by his Maker. Accordingly, it was impious and also very poor economics to pay him for gifts that he received gratis from God. So he was paid no salary. He lived on what members of his congregation in moments of similar inspiration were moved to give. However it was understood that the less inspired might require occasional prodding.

Buddhists, Hindus, sun and fire worshipers, and practitioners of voodoo and self-mortification, all a certain source of missionary expense to other denominations, also had their future fully predetermined – presumably all had been born damned. So no money need be spent on their rehabilitation. A Sunday school was redundant for the same reasons; there was no need to bring the young to the faith. They were either already there or they never would be. And, as perhaps the most inspired source of saving, there was no need for a weekly sermon. Things having already been arranged, it was unnecessary to apply constant pressure to reform the sinners or to keep the saved from backsliding. No harm would be done if a preacher came once a month and preached four times as long. This was the practice, and it meant that one man could handle four congregations. However it was understood that in practice no single sermon should much exceed an hour, and the annual deficit was made up, at least in part, by what was called May Meeting.

3

May Meeting came during the second weekend in May. Along the northern shore of Lake Erie, this is a splendid time. One can sit on the new grass and feel fully the return-ing warmth of the sun. It is the season of hepaticas and violets and jack-in-the-pulpits. Every fence corner stirs with new life. One's eyes feast on the color again after the black, gray and dull white of the winter. During May Meeting, there were services on Saturday morning and again on Saturday afternoon. Then on Sunday morning there was a devotional doubleheader – a sermon began at ten and ended at eleven and was followed immediately by another which lasted until a little after twelve. There was another service on Sunday afternoon and a final session on Monday morning which, however, was less well attended than the rest. By then many of the Scotch felt that God would wish to see them back at work. Those who attended faithfully had by the end of the Meeting six full hours of sermons to their credit. This was the equivalent of three months of ordinary half-hour exercises taken at the rate of one a week.

Nothing in these devotions would have interested a visiting Mencken. If hell-and-damnation religion were at one pole, this would be at the other. The proceedings opened with the Psalm. The congregation then sat down in the oaken pews and looked at the minister. The minister looked at the congregation and told it of its fate. The congregation heard him out in silence. My father, almost alone among the entire gathering, could manage to go to sleep. This was a feat the builder of the pews had sought to prevent or else God had guided his hand.

At some time during the weekend a number of the more committed members of the congregation accompanied Elder Slauson to the Thames River, some seven miles to the north, for baptismal ceremonies. Lake Erie was much closer but at this season it was still forbiddingly cold with awkward waves. In most years only one or two candidates, usually women of rather mature years, presented themselves and the purpose of the sacrament was something of a puzzle. Given the rigid prearrangement to which we were subject, it was hard to see how one's prospects in the next world could be improved, or for that matter usefully altered, even by the total immersion which church doctrine required. And whatever the nature of sin as seen by our church, it was certainly not soluble in river water. Doubts were, indeed, harbored. Our family never attended. Although as youngsters our curiosity was much aroused, especially over the arrangements for getting into dry clothing afterward, for at this time of the year in Canada one did not trifle with soaking wet garments however hallowed the occasion, all comment on the proceedings was firmly discouraged. As one curious consequence we were born and reared as Baptists but with the feeling that baptism was vaguely indecent.

To return to the sermons, my recollection of these exercises is of the most acute pain. For thirty years I have not been in a church for other than architectural reasons or to witness a marriage or funeral, and it is partly because I associate them to this day with torture. In Chartres, the Sainte Chapelle, Cologne, Winchester, and the great Hindu temple in Coimbatore, I have traced a vague uneasiness to the thought that I might be trapped by Elder Slauson. To this day, I never sit down to listen to a speech or a lecture without making a mental calculation as to when it will be over. That was the question that was in one's mind when those terrible sermons began, and one knew, despite whatever resources in optimism on which he might draw, that for all practical purposes they never would be. By half-closing my eyes during a dull lecture, I can to this day see the spare, dark and highly undistinguished features of that Dunwich Township divine. Once when I was eight or nine, my father gave me a dollar watch. According to local lore, they did not last long. For many months I kept mine in the box and carried it only once a month to church. This was not vanity. The sermon was a form of punishment beyond anything that hell had to offer. But it was heaven itself to look at the watch and learn that two or sometimes even three minutes had passed.

4

Above a certain age, it was partial compensation that May Meeting for the Scotch was also a considerable social event.

Some ten miles to the north around Glencoe and Ekfrid, to the northwest around Duart and Lobo were the other congregations on Elder Slauson's circuit. All were members, more or less distant, of our own clans. For May Meeting, they would drive over to our church. Many of our people would then go to the June Meeting at Ekfrid or the similar festivals at one of the other churches. Among the Scotch, it is a matter of pride to be clannish. These meetings were a major manifestation of clannishness.

The two large and related springtime tasks in households tributary to our church were spring housecleaning and getting ready for May Meeting. Before the automobile became common, a clutch of distant relatives would show up on Saturday after the services and remain through Sunday. Sleeping accommodation for the men had to be rather informal; sometimes straw would be put down in the summer kitchen. No one ever announced his arrival in advance, and it was a matter of pride to be prepared for all who might come. Ours was a small clan, rather loosely knit, and we rarely had overnight guests or more than a dozen, young and old, for Sunday dinner. The Grahams who were a large and clannish clan might have as many as forty for two days. Considerations of economy were not allowed to interfere with this hospitality even among the most penurious of the Scotch. A good man stood at his door and made everyone welcome. And the magnificent spreads of roast chicken, stuffing, gravy, homemade bread and butter, pickles, preserves and multiple choices of pie required little cash outlay. Their excellence depended not on a man's money but on the skill and energy of his wife. These last he could give with a lavish hand.

5

Between the Presbyterians and the Old School Baptists, there was a certain measure of rivalry. Numbers, prestige and general preeminence were on the side of the Presbyterians. Our church, however, included a considerable number of the loftier clans, and we gained a certain esteem from the extreme austerity of our doctrines. Like the Christian martyrs, we were thought, not inaccurately, to suffer for our beliefs. We also missed the devastating schism which rent the Presbyterians in the mid-1920s.

This was the row over church union. The union of the Protestant churches was a project that had appealed to good churchmen in Canada for many years. During World War I, men of all faiths had marched together under one God to shoot down the barbarous, although admittedly also Christian, hordes of Germany and Austria-Hungary. If men could be so united for God's work in war, surely they could be joined together in peace. Or so the argument ran.

This union did not, of course, include the Catholics. The regular Baptists declined. The Old School Baptists were not asked; our liturgy could not be readily assimilated and neither, possibly, could our pews. In the end, it came down to the Methodists, the Congregationalists and the Presbyterians. The first two voted themselves into the United Church of Canada *en bloc*, and the Presbyterians, having made a strong move in that direction, were then assailed by doubts. It was agreed to allow each congregation to vote on the matter itself. If the losers favored union they could as individuals follow their conscience into a neighboring United Church. Were it those opposing union who lost they could worship with some Presbyterian congregation that had won its election. But the church and church property went with the majority. Thus, what might have been a rather complex decision turning on difficult doctrinal points became, in the main, a quite comprehensible row over real estate. At stake in our community was the big red brick church on the Currie Road. If the unionists won, they would share it with the Methodists. The continuing Presbyterians, by appealing to a government property commission which had been established to handle such questions, might conceivably have been awarded the small Methodist frame church. If the Presbyterians won, they would keep the edifice which they and their fathers had built and paid for.

The fairness of elections is thought by many to be a matter of the morality of the people participating. Much more frequently it turns on the importance of the issues. If nothing much is at stake, men will be honest. If the issues are grave, morality will be subject to a proportionately greater strain with the increased likelihood that it will break or bend. For the Presbyterians, a great deal was at stake, and so it was a rather dirty election.

Efforts were made to influence the preacher who, in turn, was in a strategic position to influence his flock. At first, he leaned to union. Pressure was brought to bear by the large number who were opposed. He then leaned back. This infuriated the unionists who proceeded to spread the story that he had swung back only because he had observed that most pastors were for union which meant that the mediocre ones would have difficulty finding employment in the new church. The continuing Presbyterians publicly complimented him on accepting divine guidance.

Simony reared its head. Big Jack Crawford (according to rule I disguise matters for the girls survive) had three massive daughters who were neither beautiful nor musical but who yearned, as did all maidens of their age and marital hopes, to sing in the choir. Big Jack was opposed to union as he had been opposed to every innovation since the cream separator and Mary Crawford, his wife, had voiced the general belief of quite a few Presbyterians when she said that "If God had intended us to worship with the Methodists, He would have had us do it in the first place." But the unionists got to Jack's daughters and offered them places in the choir. The girls worked on Jack; he knew that his life would be hideous if he did not yield. Too late the continuing Presbyterians learned what was happening and came through with counter promises. The Crawfords all voted for union.

There was the more regrettable case of Annie McTavish. Her husband, Malcolm, had died some years before. A gentle soul and a faithful member of the kirk, he had been treated badly by his wife. As often happens, she assuaged her conscience by an excess of affection after his death. She told often and publicly of how she looked forward to lying by Malcolm's side beneath the modest McTavish headstone. She was then in her late seventies.

Annie's children were in favor of union. She was said to be leaning that way. But as the balloting week approached, it became less and less certain that this was the winning side. A delegation of non-concurring Presbyterians, as they were generally termed throughout the Dominion, called on Annie and told her that if they won, she could never lie by Malcolm's side. As a supporter of the United Church she could not rest in Presbyterian soil. Annie indignantly denounced these tactics and promptly proclaimed her intention of voting with her offspring for "the Union." Deep in her heart she had always abhorred the thought of keeping company with Malcolm's mouldering bones.

In the end, union was decisively defeated. A little band of liberals moved over to the Methodists and after a few years raised enough money to cover the outside of the church with red brick. Our church, meanwhile, went on in its ascetic way. We neither gained nor lost strength from the troubles of our fellow Protestants. But it was considered by all an interesting election.

6

The schism mirrored rather accurately the religious tendencies of the Scotch. As I have noted, no question of doctrine was raised. Save as a source of political pressure on the preacher, God did not enter the dispute. But the church was very much at issue.

The Scotch thought well of their churches both as institutions and as pieces of property. They enjoyed the feeling of membership that came from appearing with their offspring in their accustomed place each Sabbath morning. They felt a trifle more akin to those clansmen who were members of their own congregation than to others. They attached rather more credence to the intelligence on markets, crop prospects, the weather outlook or the last speech by Sir Wilfrid Laurier or Mr. William Lyon Mackenzie

King that was communicated to them after church than to anything that was picked up on a purely secular occasion. The after-church colloquia of the Scotch were indeed notable affairs. Elder Slauson would usually relent a little after noon. Thereupon, the congregation adjourned to the church grounds. No man of more than minimal curiosity ever started home before one.

In contrast with this feeling of comfortable affection inspired by the church, the Scotch were a trifle uneasy about God. He was never mentioned, save by the profane, in ordinary conversation. Farming in Southern Ontario was more than normally subject to the weather. The weather, to a singular degree, is of heavenly manufacture. Yet none of our neighbors would have dreamed of appealing to God for relief from a drought or for dry weather for the bean harvest. Every once in a while a well-meaning minister, perhaps a visitor from town who was standing in for a regular divine, would take note of the damage being done by a prolonged dry spell and ask for rain. His terrestrial audience, to the extent that they were listening, would attribute the request to a lack of farm experience. Certainly they did not expect it to do any good. A few Scotch were obliged by the custom of their clan to say grace at mealtimes. And, on occasion, the principal Man of Standing would be asked to perform a similar office at a family reunion or at dinner before a funeral. This was done in haste and with poorly concealed embarrassment and in the case of my father, when he was called, without any knowledge whatever of the words. The intonation which was as standardized as the Anglican Book of Common Prayer, went as follows:

Lord for these blesssssss sss
Ssss sss sss sss sss ss.
Ssss sss sss sss ssssss
Ssss sss ssist sake. Amen

It was assumed that God could render it into English if he wished.

It is possible that the Scotch had a deeper relation to God than here appears but this I doubt. They did not ask God for anything they could do for themselves or, as a practical matter, for anything they couldn't do for themselves and didn't expect to get done. I have told of a neighbor who got late to his fields because of his morning devotions. From the point of view of the community, there couldn't have been a worse reason. If God made sense, he didn't want a man staying around the house when he should have been out on his land.

Some will deplore such a secular community, will say that something of spiritual importance was missing. Perhaps. But this could be a parochial and inaccurate view. As matters are regarded from heaven, the proper vantage point, there must be some merit in people who look after themselves, do not request the impossible and keep to an absolute minimum the number of purely ritualistic and ceremonial petitions. Certainly there is much to be said for the reticence of the Scotch in their relations with God. Macaulay once spoke with repugnance of the recurring spasms of British concern for popular morals. We have our similar bouts of public piety. The last occurred during the Eisenhower Administration. Public figures were regularly pictured in rapt communication with the Creator. Cabinet meetings were opened by a prayer by Ezra Taft Benson, a public servant with an unparalleled absence of public compassion who subsequently blessed, at least partially, the doctrines of the John Birch Society without any evident concern as to how these might be reconciled with injunctions to compassion, charity and the Golden Rule. The Scotch would not have approved this public display of piety. They would have wondered if prayer was being used as a cover for some evasion of earthly duty. They would have been right to ask.

X

The Urban Life

I f one went east on Hogg Street for a little under three miles to where it met the Southwold Townline, he came to our nearest market center, Iona Station. Here the railroads, the Canada Southern become the double-tracked Michigan Central, then the New York Central and paralleled by the single line of the Pere Marquette (since the Chesapeake and Ohio), came in at an angle across the countryside and also crossed the Townline. It was this intersection of roads and railroads which had made the place. In earlier years, life had centered on another community two miles nearer the Lake, Iona by name, but the railroads had missed it, and it had gone into decline. Iona Station had risen in its place.

It was a pleasant community with a sound basic plan. At one side of town, where Hogg Street met the Townline, and a little apart from both the commercial and industrial areas, was the religious and cultural center. North along the principal street, one came first to the residential section and then the main shopping center with the service industries conveniently close. After that came the railroads, the railroad stations, stockyards, another small residential area, another shopping center and a small manufacturing establishment. A good half mile north of town, intelligently remote from all urban influences, was the school. Maples shaded the mercantile, manufacturing and residential areas alike; people walked not on harsh asphalt but on grass. No activity or function of the town intruded itself on any other save that, of a night, people might be momentarily aroused by a passing train. No one resented this for, potentially at least, the railroads provided as fine a system of communications as that of any community in the world. Were one to step on a train, one could proceed westward without changing cars to Windsor, Detroit and Chicago. A single change would bring him to San Francisco, and the gateway to the Orient. To the east, he could go with equal convenience to Niagara Falls, Buffalo, Syracuse, Albany and New York City. With a single change from train to ship, he could be on to Liverpool, Southampton or Glasgow.

Unfortunately, the trains did not stop. Largely for this reason, Iona Station, the diversity of its economic life notwithstanding, was very small – in my time not more than twenty-five souls. The cultural center comprised a white brick church and a small frame hall used for box socials, an occasional political meeting and, in later and morally more relaxed times, an infrequent dance. (The Scotch were divided on dancing, Highland dancing apart. An older and sterner generation held it to be wicked and likely to divert attention from serious labor. But the moderate majority now approved of it in moderation.) The church served a very small congregation, and its architect had solved a difficult problem in an interesting way. No matter how small it is, a church must have a certain minimum height – there must be headroom for the people and religious dignity requires a certain altitude. Since the building needed to accommodate only a handful of people, he had reduced its length until it slightly resembled a small pancake stood on edge. By the time of this study, the church was served only by an itinerant divine. The residential section consisted of four or five frame houses all in need of paint. John Dundas, a very good blacksmith, provided a universal repair service all by himself. The Pere Marquette station stood empty, a monument to unrealized commercial hopes, and one day the company loaded it on a flatcar and carried it away. The stockyards were also in decline. The store to the north of the tracks was financially insecure, and after one fire had been put out by the neighbors it was carried away by a second. Manufacturing was in the hands of an aged harness-maker whose enterprise was also sadly athwart the march of technology. One could still buy a ticket on the mail and accommodation trains at the Michigan Central Station, and the stationmaster was a man of consequence. But for all practical purposes, Iona Station consisted of Dan McBride's store.

2

McBride's was almost though not quite everything that a country store should be. It was a low story-and-a-half building with a porch, a hitching rail out front and signs celebrating Cow Brand Baking Soda, Salada Tea and the Clan McBride. It was built of wood and could also have done with a coat of paint. On each side of the door was a window which admitted a certain amount of light into one end of what, architecturally, was a square tunnel. On the counter on the left as one entered was a candy case, fly specked and rather dusty but with a colorful array of all-day suckers, peppermint candy and chocolate bars. The counter extended on protecting shelves of canned goods and boxes of crackers, sugar, flour, dates, prunes, and other comestibles. Perched on the inner end of the counter was the post office, a small barricade of mail boxes with a wicket in the middle. (In past times the post office had been an important piece of patronage. But instead of the new man moving in to the post office after an election, the post office was moved in with the new postmaster. This could be accomplished in half an hour or so. Opposite the grocery department was apparel and hardware – overalls, smocks, ginghams, lanterns, lamp chimneys, yellow sweat pads for horses, straw hats, leather gloves, woolen mittens, hoes, rakes, and much else. The whole establishment was heated by a big wood stove at the back. The smell was dominated by codfish and kerosene (coal oil it was called) and was rather pleasant. Much has been written of the deeply satisfying aroma of the country store. Few have understood that its attraction was less in itself than in what it replaced. Any strong scent that similarly masked the less elegant odors of everyday life would have been similarly celebrated. Among Dan McBride's patrons were a number who made the smell of codfish and kerosene more than normally welcome.

Dan McBride was a quiet, mild-mannered man of medium height and undistinguished appearance. He was known to have made quite a bit of money out of the store for he was a well-regarded source of mortgage money for anyone buying a farm. Apart from his money, he was in every respect an average citizen.

Hannah, his wife, was a woman of much more marked personality. Spare, sallow, rather sharp-featured with gray-brown hair, complexion and attire, she was, at a certain level, perhaps the best-informed woman in the two townships. Her specialty was human frailty and personal disaster. If someone had consumption, a quarrel with his brother, brother-in-law or hired man, was afraid that her last baby was not quite bright, or had been thrown in front of a disk harrow by an unruly horse, you heard about it first from Hannah. Once, no doubt, she had passed along these grim tidings with a certain appearance of sorrow. But she was an honest soul, and in time she abandoned pretense and came to issue her bulletins with the joy she really felt.

The talk in a country store is known to be good – sage, amusing, colorful and rich in its perception of human nature. But in this respect Dan McBride's was below par, and this may well have been the case with most country stores. On winter evenings, men came through the deep snow to sit around the stove at the back of the store. And in the summer, the same crowd gathered on the porch or by the hitching rail in front. If No. 6 had come through late, the tardiness would be duly noted. Had it been hot or cold, this fact would be recorded together, perhaps, with comparative thermometer readings. Birth, morbidity and death of men and animals were established fare. So were farming operations. There wasn't much else. Here, as in most gatherings, tired men favored the topics not that engaged the mind but that freed it from all pretense of effort.

But there were other reasons for the commonplace quality of the discussions around the stove. McBride's was the club of the nonmembers. The Men of Standing would not dream of going there for an evening. They couldn't have it said they were wasting the time. Nor would they have been entirely welcome, for their rank would have required them to dominate the conversation. Nor did the average clansman attend; he was not impelled to look for company after the sun went down. He might drop in briefly on a neighbor; more likely he reflected with brief contentment on the completion of the day's labors and went to bed. It was the hired men, an occasional section hand, the mail carrier, those who farmed an exceptionally recalcitrant stretch of land to the south of town who went to Dan McBride's. These, the outcasts and the untouchables, gathered for mutual sustenance and support. They didn't say much that was important for, as they well knew, they weren't supposed by the community to have anything important to say.

3

Although for its size, Iona Station had a certain economic diversity, there were limits to its commercial resources. For the considerable range of implements and supplies that their agriculture required, for most of the goods which their modest standard of living allowed, and for advanced education, the

Scotch turned to a much more imposing center, the village of Dutton. This could be approached from our place in two ways. One could turn north over Willey's Sideroad, in the direction opposite from the school, pass the Camerons', cross the railroads and then turn west by McFarlanes', McCurdys', McIntyres' and the famous Hereford farms of the McNeils and come into town on Shackleton Street, socially the most distinguished avenue in town. It was not necessarily the most comfortable. The railroads, in their angular passage, had now drawn over to this road. As a product of a plausible process of social history, the oldest and hence the most distinguished families lived in the oldest part of town. That, not unnaturally, was the part closest to the railroads where the town began. The price of social pre-eminence, therefore, was to suffer the Michigan Central express trains which went thundering through a few yards away. They did not stop at Dutton either.

One could also go straight up Hogg Street and instead of turning left on the Currie Road to Wallacetown, turn right by the Grahams', the Fairview Cemetery, past the McVicars' and again into town.

On this approach, one came first to a small foundry and machine shop which, with the coming of the automobile, became Dutton's leading garage. Few things were ever more ardently debated by the Scotch than whether a Ford performed better or worse after remedial action at this establishment. It is exceedingly doubtful if there was any improvement but neither was there any alternative. And though the fact is now largely forgotten, the Model T Ford lent itself to a treatment that was essentially psychiatric in character. It might refuse to start except after the most formidable exercise of choking and cranking or, as was the practice in our neighborhood, after being hauled down the road in high gear by a horse. Or it might develop a major irregularity of gait or weaken alarmingly on the hills. The owner, experienced only with animals, thereupon took it to a garageman who also did not know what was wrong. But out of the discussion of the probable disorder and the discovery of common ignorance came a measure of reassurance. The operator learned that others had similar troubles and that his management was not to blame. And it was the inimitable quality of this particular machine that whatever went wrong was almost invariably healed by time and further use.

Across from the garage was a slovenly frame building where someone had once started a laundry. It was also said that an optimistic entrepreneur had once imported talent with a view to setting up a very small-scale whore house. Since the relative values attached to love and money by the rural Scotch were well known, it is hard to see how he could have expected to make much income. Perhaps it went back to the building or double-tracking of the railroad. In any case, the building retained an unsavory reputation, and the better class of people deliberately looked the other way when they went past.

Next came the railroad tracks protected by gates, a tower and a gateman. The latter, like many men with nothing to do, was rarely without help. The railroad had a strict rule against anyone coming into his tower but he interpreted it as excluding only those who could beat him at checkers or who could not play. Beyond the tracks, Main Street proper began. It was bare, unshaded, unadorned and very unattractive.

The buildings were of red or white brick with square façades, sometimes with the date of construction decorating the second story. They were a parody on the buildings on a thousand Main Streets in North America and it is doubtful if, as a builder, man has ever done worse on a comparable scale. In front of the buildings ran a double-width sidewalk. Between that and the street was an iron horse rail. These survived the horses for many years for they were principally used as a perch for people coming to town.

The west side of Main Street was the high-rent side. First after the tracks, somewhat unfairly in the view of the local merchants, came a large billboard advertising Dowler's haberdashery in the neighboring city of St. Thomas. Here also was a small white brick building which housed the clerk of the Township of Dunwich and a dirty white frame build-ing, with the usual false front, which housed *The Dutton Advance*. *The Advance* was a weekly consisting partly of advertisements, partly of local news supplied by correspon-dents in exchange for the literary opportunity and a free subscription, and partly of singularly unreadable boiler plate. The local news had to be set by hand and, for reasons of economy, was kept to a minimum. *The Advance* had no editorials and hence no editorial policy. This also saved on typesetting but it was otherwise a sensible decision. Everyone who owns a paper imagines that he has ideas which are both important and influential. In the nature of things, there must be exceptions, and J. D. Blue, who owned *The Advance*, was one of the few newspaper proprietors to realize that he might be one. Feeling that the Scotch would not have thought his ideas on any subject of the slightest value, he did not offer them.

After *The Advance* came Herb Hale's butcher shop, Hodder's bakery and ice cream parlor, Dan Black's real estate office (farm properties), Panter's store which combined dry-goods with groceries, Crawford's hardware which combined groceries with hardware and then the T. Hockin Company, Ltd., Dutton's most pretentious emporium, which combined almost everything except hardware with a grocery department. After that in a succession of two-story brick-fronted buildings came the Royal Bank of Canada, the long since defunct Molson's Bank, Roberts' Drug Store (Friendly Rexall Service), Bambridge's Jewellery (Signet, birthstone, lodge rings; watch, jewellery and spectacle repair), a candy store, assorted other vendors, a barbershop, a poolroom, and at the end the Queen's Hotel. The latter was an extremely barren red brick structure which housed the hotelkeeper's family and no one else. A different family took up residence every year or so.

4

The opposite side of Main Street was commercially less impressive but culturally more interesting. More or less across from the Queen's Hotel was the red brick community hall. This had replaced a smaller white brick building after World War I and had been built as a memorial to the fallen of the area. An acidulous relative of ours, reflecting the common view of the Scotch of this conflict, said it was the only proof that they had not died in vain. However from an architectural point of view, this was debatable.

The east side of Main Street also had an interesting black-smith shop conducted by a dour craftsman called Bill Affleck and, in addition, a doctor, lawyer, dentist, the county agent (in Ontario styled the Agricultural Representative), a haber-dashery, a farm implement and automobile salesroom, another baker, another grocer, another barber, and the McIntyre House.

The McIntyre House was, by all odds, the most interesting establishment in town.

XI

The McIntyre House

The McIntyre house stood nearly in the center of the east side of the single block that comprised Main Street. Unlike the square brick-fronted buildings across and on either side, it was longer, lower and of frame construction. Once it had been white with green trim, and traces of the original paint remained. At the north end was an arch cut through the building which gave access to the livery stables behind and to another blacksmith shop run by Jim Bruce who, on all festival occasions and for a moderate fee, closed his shop, donned the ancient tartan of the Bruce and took up his pipes to provide the only music the Scotch understood and loved. Also in the hotel yard were the privies, a massive bank of cells, undifferentiated as to sex or precision of user, each cell giving on to a single trench which was cleaned out only at infrequent intervals. They gave off an astonishing smell. Immediately adjacent was the kitchen.

However, it was not for its food that the McIntyre House was renowned but its drink. A door within the arch led into the bar; there was another in from the street. In the 1920s this valiant room was already in decline; pool tables had been moved in to retrieve, however ingloriously, some of the revenues that had once accrued exclusively to whisky. But the scars of the greater days could still be seen on the wainscotting, the doors and deep in the bar itself. Before prohibition came to Ontario in 1916, it had been the resort of the drinking Scotch. As the result, it had been the scene of some of the most uproarious violence that alcohol has ever produced.

The effect of alcohol on different races is as remarkable as it is invariable. An Englishman becomes haughty; a Swede sad; an Irishman sentimental; a Russian fraternal; a German melodious. A Scotchman always becomes militant. It was on Saturday night that the Scotch gathered at the McIntyre House to make merry and seek one another's destruction. Whisky bottles were emptied and used as weapons; sometimes the bottom was knocked off to make a better impression on the thick epidermis that so admirably protected the average clansman. Boots and even furniture were also used, although on gala occasions the furniture was removed. On a Sunday after one of these festivals, men would be in poor condition from Port Talbot to Campbellton and from Iona Station nearly to West Lorne.

Even among the nondrinking Scotch, the tales of the McIntyre House were part of the legend. Once a commercial traveler from Toronto had called for a cocktail and gave instructions on how to make it. The patrons were outraged but Johnnie McIntyre quieted them down and went out for ice. This he got from a little iceberg by a tree in the yard. It owed its origins to the dogs who frequented the tree and to the Canadian winter which quickly converted all moisture to ice. Johnnie thought this would return the man to whisky and so did those to whom he quietly confided the stratagem. The man from Toronto praised the flavor and called for another.

There was also the night that my great-uncle Duncan, then the family ambassador to the drinking Scotch, sat next to one of the McPherson boys who had begun to worry lest whisky was getting the better of him. After once again confiding sadly of his fears, he drank a large bottle of carbolic acid. To the surprise of all who had known his capacity, he died a horrible death.

Finally, there was the gala evening – it must have been about 1910 – when one of the Campbells who inhabited the country north and west of town mounted the bar and announced his intention of avenging, once and for all, the insults that had been heaped on the Clan Campbell ever since it had fought on the wrong side at Culloden a hundred and sixty-five years before. He specifically promised to lick any man who lived between Lake Erie and the Michigan Central Railway. A score leaped to the challenge; the Campbells rallied round. It was a glorious struggle. The outcome was indeterminate although it was said that the Campbells acquitted themselves well. Next morning a half-dozen clansmen were still stacked like cordwood in the livery stable back of the hotel. None was seriously hurt.

2

Prohibition was advocated in Ontario partly as a product of the natural desire of better men to impose their virtue on the worse. But partly it was considered an important pacifying influence which would raise markedly the productivity of the farm labor force. The slogan of the prohibitionists, "Abolish the bar," showed the way in which their concern had become associated not with whisky but with the theater of combat. Prohibition came and when it was later repealed in Ontario, the principal concern was not to control the intake of alcohol but to insure that it occurred in surroundings which were inconsistent with physical violence. This the institution of the cocktail lounge accomplished.

Once the bar of the McIntyre House was closed, the Scotch deserted it in droves. The poolroom was taken over by the idlers of the town and no good was thought to come of anyone who frequented the place. In point of fact, none did.

Commercial travelers must have stopped at the McIntyre House. Certainly a horse-drawn bus went down to meet each train at the MCR station. Occasionally one of the girls of the town who worked there as chambermaid would be seen leaning out an upstairs window exchanging insults with a boy friend in the street. In the main lobby adjoining the bar was a desk and a yellowed and dog-eared guest register. Out back was the dining room. But in its days of glory, the McIntyre House meant the bar. The rest must have been operated as an afterthought.

3

I have memory of only one moment when the McIntyre House was in its glory. It must have been on the first of July of 1914 or 1915 when I was approaching the age of either six or seven. We had gone to Dutton to celebrate Dominion Day, the Canadian Fourth of July, and to attend the Caledonian games. There had been running and broad-jumping, and throwing of weights for distance and height, and a great deal of sword dancing and piping. Some of the dancing we found tedious but the rest was wholly fascinating. My father, one of the officials of the West Elgin Caledonian Society, had looked very grand in a modified kilt of the McDonald tartan – not many of the clansmen owned a complete kilt so they made do with what they had. Then at four o'clock my sister and I were bundled into the family democrat, a large four-wheeled affair with a fringed top, and we started for home because word had come that the fighting had begun. As we passed the McIntyre House, we saw it. Some forty or fifty clansmen, the drinking Scotch at nearly their maximum effective strength, had been reinforced by elements of a Scottish regiment which had come to grace the celebration and provide music. Some of the celebrants were in the bar; others were struggling to approach it or shouting to those inside to pass out the bottles. A number of fights were already in progress in the crowd outside; from within came joyful shrieks and loud crashes indicating that hostilities were much more advanced inside. Pipers around the edge of the struggling mass were offering a competitive combination of pibrochs, marches and laments to inspire the combatants to greater feats of violence. We got by as quickly as the traffic and our alarmed mare would allow.

We drove down Shackleton Street and across Willey's Sideroad, and the memory of that journey on a summer evening by the bare hayfields and through the fields of ripening wheat has never forsaken me. The sound of the pipes did not recede and fade; on the contrary, it grew in volume as the whisky was passed out and the pipers warmed to their work. And at intervals, over the spiel of the pipes came the high demoniac shrieks which for a thousand years on ten thousand battlefields has struck terror to the hearts of the brave. It is the cry of uncontrollable joy of a drunken Highlander as he rushes toward personal immolation.

A year or two later, the McIntyre House was selling nothing more dangerous than Orange Crush.

4

The pavement stopped at the end of the business section by the town hall. A gravel road led on by the tiny office of the veterinary surgeon, in front of which on fine days the good doctor could be seen tipped back in his chair resting. A stout, amiable and only moderately intelligent man, he was much respected in the community for his good humor and his devotion to patriotic causes. On Dominion Day, Armistice Day and the anniversaries of other occasions important in Canadian annals, he willingly chaired committees and gave his energies selflessly to the arrangements. There may have been something compulsive about this, a lurking need to compensate, for he was an American citizen.

At a bend in the road was the Baptist Church; beyond that were the frame houses of the lesser merchants and the clergy and then came the public school, Hollingshead's mill where we sold our wheat and had our oats ground or rolled and beyond that the Dutton High School. The High School played a large role in the important, complex, and wholly fascinating interaction between town and country to which I now turn.

XII

Higher Education

The Dutton High School in those days was a gaunt two-story building of white brick and hideous aspect. It stood in a small yard in which only ragweed and plantain reliably survived the dense foot traffic. Land in Canada is plentiful and inexpensive and thus not highly regarded. So only a few square yards are provided for a school. In England where it is scarce and costly and much admired several acres of playing fields would have been considered a minimum.

The school had a front door that was reserved for girls and a back door that was available to either sex. No one ever explained the reason for this rule or its contribution to adolescent purity for we led a fully integrated existence once inside. Beyond the back door was a well and pump. There was no baseball diamond, no basketball hoop, no football posts, not even a pond for ice hockey. Our protection from the socialist interdependence inculcated by the team spirit continued to be complete.

The only relief from the barrenness of the yard and the board fences that surrounded it was provided by nice trees which provided some shade and two outdoor toilets. A friend of mine, the son of one of the fishing families by the Lake, could stand in the middle of one of these and pee out of a window a good six feet distant and a full five feet up from the floor. It never did him any good in after life, poor fellow, for after graduation he got a job with the local branch of the Royal Bank and was sent to jail shortly thereafter for walking out with several thousand dollars. This was not the crime that it might seem. The big Canadian banks tested their new employees by having them work with considerable sums for practically no compensation. An occasional failure was inherent in the system.

2

Autobiography is famous for the odd figures that it parades across the pages of literature. But anthropology also has its accidental specimens. In the interests of science it is now necessary to accord immortality of a kind to the unexpectant memory of Mr. Thomas Elliott, principal of the Dutton High School for several decades in the first half of the twentieth century.

Old Tommy, as he was known unaffectionately by many generations of adolescents, was a man of a little more than medium height and of substantial though not stocky build. He must have been in his early fifties in the middle 1920s and he carefully combed his sparse gray hair, which had something of the appearance of crab grass in a dry autumn, over his bald spot with an increasing absence of plausibility. His face was full and covered by a gray, unhealthy skin and, although he shaved every day, slight gray wisps always survived between the swaths. In the winter he wore a dark gray suit of hard, very shiny, very durable material; in the summer he changed the jacket for one of lighter gray. In many men this predominant gray in hair, complexion and attire would have left one with the impression of a colorless personality. In Old Tommy the impression was countered by the appearance and employment of his eyes and mustache.

Both of these were full and dark and they worked in unison. Before addressing you, Old Tommy partly closed his right eye and brought it down toward the corner of his mustache in what was evidently intended to be a look of infinite guile. At the same time, perhaps more accidentally, the mustache rose up to meet the eye. This remarkable configuration he could hold for an indefinite time while he transfixed you with the full force of his left eye. Then he addressed you. In the young this exercise aroused a quavering fear. It was a mark of maturity when it came only to inspire mistrust.

In any calling Old Tommy would have been counted a man of remarkable ignorance but as an educator he excelled. As one of four teachers, three of whom happily were always better, since they couldn't have been worse, he taught geography, spelling, zoology, physics and chemistry. In all of these, with the possible exception of spelling, he was grossly uninformed.

In matters unrelated to pedagogy Old Tommy was equally uninstructed. The 1920s were years of much excitement in Canada. As noted following the war, the farmers rose in righteous anger over their high costs and falling prices and installed their own government, the United Farmers of Ontario, in Toronto. In Ottawa ministries rose and fell. All the most respectable people had invested their moral and political capital in the war. Now after the expenditure of hundreds of millions of dollars and tens of thousands of lives they seemed as uncertain as everyone else about what had been accomplished. Few escaped blame. General Sir Arthur William Currie, Canada's most famous soldier, was honored on his return with the post of Principal of McGill University and shortly thereafter found himself in court (as result of a libel case) denying that he had contributed unnecessarily to the butchery of Canadian soldiers on the Western Front. (It was as though Ike, having gone to Columbia University as its president, had been forced on to the stand by his detractors on his management of the Battle of the Bulge. He would not have liked it.) Railways were nationalized in these years. The highways were laid out across the Ontario mud. Women got the vote. Old Tommy would often express an opinion on these events but we knew even as youngsters that it was worthless. We never cited it at home for we also knew that it provoked a serious conflict between two strongly held beliefs of the Men of Standing among the Scotch. Nothing should ever be said at home that undermined a schoolmaster's authority. Equally, people should know what they were talking about.

3

On one thing Old Tommy made a certain approach to competence. That was in exploiting the dislike between the people of the village, who more than incidentally controlled the school, and the ordinary citizens among the rural Scotch. This skill had something to do with his survival.

Every community must have some form of social conflict. Harmony is praised in principle and by the clergy but faction is what people really enjoy. It gives a welcome sense of companionship to those on the same side; it arouses no less than organized athletics or aggressive nationalism the competitive ardor of those involved. The important thing is not to avoid such conflict but to guide it on to issues where it does no damage to life and limb or the real income of the community. The conflict between town and country in our community was probably as benign as any that careful planning could have contrived.

The Scotch disliked the townspeople partly for reasons of race. They did not, on the whole, think as well of the English as of themselves and quite a few of the leading citizens of the town were English and even supported – it was thought by some out of sheer snobbishness – a small Anglican church. But this was only a partial cause for the Scotch had established strong outposts in the village: John McCallum was the tailor and operated an informal club for the Men of Standing; Johnny Campbell sold Massey-Harris implements and Ford cars; Johnny McIntyre had been the Delmonico of the drinking Scotch; John Archie McNeil was the undertaker; Douglas Galbraith was the doctor.

Politics played some role. The merchants were Tories in politics; the Scotch with rare exceptions were Liberals. They disliked having their votes cancelled out by people who did not use the franchise intelligently. But there were also numerous Scotch Liberals in town.

Economic determinism had more to do with the struggle. Contemplating the considerable well-being of the elder Hockin, a Scotch farmer could only conclude that it was the result of buying cheap and selling dear. It could not be attributed to harder work; running a store was obviously easier than running a farm. Superior intelligence would not be conceded. Tom, it was evident, had got rich at the expense of the farmers. And the merchants had a reciprocal grievance. The farmers gave a lot of business to the great Toronto mail order houses of Messrs. T. Eaton Co. and Robert Simpson & Co. This showed a callous lack of appreciation for the efforts of the local merchants to supply good merchandise at reasonable prices. It also overlooked the elementary economic truth that a dollar spent at home does ten times as much good as a dollar spent abroad, especially to the man who gets it.

But mostly the conflict resolved itself, as most such conflicts do, into a difference of opinion as to who was superior. The Scotch believed, I have always thought rightly, that they were. They considered agriculture an inherently superior vocation. It placed a man in his fit relation to nature; it abjured the artificialities of urban existence. It gave him peace and independence. It was morally superior for it required manual labor. The finest aphorism of the Scotch was: "A good man isn't afraid of work." Not one of them believed that clerking in a store or weighing in at an elevator was work.

The people of the town, like most urban dwellers through history, regarded the farmers as unkempt rustics to whom, for reasons of commercial expediency, they had to be affable. Veblen's system of social precedence based on exemption from manual toil they would have regarded as sound. To sell drygoods or serve as chief executive of the livery stable was an undoubted mark of superiority or should have been.

An aristocracy that is accepted comprises, without doubt, the most contented of men. But privilege to be completely pleasant must be above dispute. No one is to be less envied than the aristocrat whose position is not conceded. And no one is to be more pitied than the man whose nobility is known only to himself. The Indian princes – Nizam, Maharana, Maharajas, Nabobs, Rajahs – were once very happy men. Their unchallenged distinction was affirmed to them in varied and elaborate ceremony by their far from reluctant subjects a hundred times a day. But democratic India has ceased to be conscious of their grandeur. The princes must explain to the visitor that their house was enti-tled by the British to a nineteen-gun salute and then what is worse they must explain the system of salutes, for the visitor does not even know about that. This is all very difficult and they are, on the whole, a subdued and saddened caste. Quite a few have abandoned the effort to sustain an aristocratic position and, depending on taste and talent, have taken refuge in either democratic politics or alcohol.

The Dutton merchants were also an unappreciated aris-tocracy. They could have survived the suspicion and dislike of the average clansman. But the Scotch had their own hier-archy. The Men of Standing, the clansmen who dominated the Scottish community and ran the township and county, stood for parliament and gave sanction to the views which others applauded and adopted. They ignored the burghers of the town. They did not defer to the political views of Tom Hockin. They did not credit him with any of importance. But here Old Tommy re-enters the picture. He was a townsman to the core. No New Yorker out of O. Henry, Horatio Alger or Damon Runyon was more passionately devoted to the urban way of life and the town party controlled the school. So, singlehandedly he set out to redress the balance in favor of his side by making life hideous for the children of the rural Scotch. Since it was the more prominent clans which principally patronized the school he was able to register his fire on those who, in the opinion of his party, were most in need of being reduced a peg or two.

4

Some years ago I became involved in a controversy with the then congressman from Georgia, Mr. Gene Cox. I was taken to task by another congressman, Mr. Joseph Starnes of Alabama, for becoming involved with his fellow southerner. "You have no business biting at Ole Gene," he said. "He is the nicest mean man in the House of Representatives." Although Old Tommy was not considered nice by anyone, he had invented – or more likely, by the simple empiricism of trial and error had chanced upon – some remarkably effective forms of meanness. What was more remarkable, all could be employed with an outward aspect of reasonableness.

Thus Old Tommy had learned that reasonable and equal laws when applied to individuals in unequal situations can have a highly unequal and wholly indefensible effect which, since the laws are reasonable, will usually go unnoticed. He had also learned that equal laws, unequally applied, can also be quite discriminatory and he did not hesitate to resort to such outright favoritism when that was indicated. He was not legalistic or hidebound in any respect.

As an example of impeccable laws with unequal effect, there was the elementary matter of promptness. It is right to insist on it in the young. Old Tommy did so and this contributed to his reputation as a wise if stern disciplinarian. But promptness presented a radically different and easier problem for town dwellers as compared with the rural Scotch. The youth of the town awoke, dressed, had breakfast and walked a few hundred yards to school. The time required for all of these acts with the possible exception of the awakening was subject to strict control. The offspring of the rural Scotch got out of bed, fed and groomed a horse, breakfasted, harnessed the horse, hitched it to a buggy or cutter, drove from two to seven miles to town, unhitched and stabled the horse somewhere near the school and then made their way to the academy on foot. A remarkable number of mishaps might occur in this sequence: a horse might be lame; traces could break in the mud; cutters could tip in the deep snow; once as the result of a moment's carelessness a mare walked off without us and made her way some four miles to Mrs. Crawford's stable – Mrs. Crawford was the dowager of the Dutton hardware hierarchy – where we rented a stall. To be covered against all such accidents one would have had to start at midnight. Every morning some of the adolescent Scotch were late and, inevitably, a few were prone. Old Tommy cherished these derelictions; he prepared his insults as other pedagogues (but not Old Tommy) prepared their lessons. After this complicated passage, we also arrived smelling a little, or more than a little, of horses, harness and stable. After an articulate analysis of the cultural deficiencies which caused us to be late, Tommy in his greater moments would go on to deal with the smell. The remarkable contortion of eyebrow, eye and mustache could, with only a minor variation, be made into a violent reaction to an offensive odor. Occasionally some especially serious offender would be sent to the pump to purify himself. He would return unimproved, as Tommy could foretell and would point out, for nothing less than total immersion would have made any difference.

Tommy's most ingenious assault on the children of the rural Scotch concerned, curiously enough, the matter of military preparedness. At the time of World War I, in one of those aberrations to which the military mind in all countries is recurrently subject, corps of cadets were organized in the Canadian high schools. A subsidy was paid for every teenager so trained. However training is not the word; in many of the schools, including that of Dutton, there was no one with the slightest military experience to give instruction. So the latter was provided by the principal, or even by an older student, after reading and placing his own very original construction on the manual of infantry drill.

It seems possible that even Old Tommy realized that these exercises were without any practical consequence. But the subsidy slightly reduced the school tax and besides being a stern disciplinarian, he was well regarded by the school trustees for his extreme penuriousness. Accordingly, twice a week, on Tuesday and Thursday mornings, the male students had close-order drill. At twenty minutes before ten we made our way upstairs and equipped ourselves with a leather army belt and a Ross rifle or its more important remnants. The Ross rifle was the weapon with which the earliest Canadian participants in World War I had been equipped. Under conditions of practical combat it was discovered, not without cost to the individuals most immediately concerned, that it did not work. It was replaced, along with nearly all of the men who had carried it, and the pieces still available were used for training. With time many of these had lost their bolts and the sights had been brushed off. So armed and formed in a ragged line with the big seventeen-year-olds at one end and the infinitesimal twelve-year-olds at the other we marched back and forth across the front yard while Old Tommy shouted the cadence.

At least the boys from the town and a few of the more adaptable of the Scotch marched back and forth.

The rest of us had trouble. A farm boy early learns to accommodate his step to that of animals – to cows coming up the lane or to horses pulling a harrow. This is not a stride but an effortless saunter which one can sustain, if necessary, all day. To convert from this to marching tempo, or rather to Old Tommy's particular interpretation of the military choreography, was for many of us impossible. After two or three paces we would be out of step; thereafter we would be back in step only as our unique cycle brought us into momentary harmony with our neighbors. That one kept in step was, perhaps, the only thing that Old Tommy really understood about military drill.

Our difficulties gave him his finest hour. Our inability to keep step he identified with acute and irremediable inferiority. And our easily suspected dislike of drill he denounced as not only seditious but damaging to the financial well-being of the community. The hopeless cases (of which I was invariably one) were put into a special formation that was formally and not inaccurately designated the Awkward Squad. Old Tommy would then turn the more tractable soldiers over to one of the fifth formers and concentrate on us. We would straggle across the yard for four or five minutes and then halt for ten while Tommy told us of our deficiencies. Believing, correctly, that an inability to concentrate our minds on our extremities had something to do with our handicaps, he would send us home night after night with the requirement that we write out five hundred times the simple declamatory sentence: *My left foot is not my right!*

For one brief moment each spring Old Tommy would forego aggression. For then we would be visited by a resplendent colonel from a regiment in London, Ontario, whose task it was to see if the school had earned the subsidy and how much. The amount depended on the number marching for the inspection and it would become evident to Old Tommy that pleasant as it all had been we still could not march. So the utterly hopeless cases, of which I was still one, would be seated on a bench, complete with leather belt, and told to explain if asked that we had been sick or lame. When enlisting us in this conspiracy against the public treasury,

Old Tommy would be almost kind – his eye and mustache would come together not in their usual alarming manner but in what was evidently meant to be a knowing wink.

In practice we were never asked. Old Tommy's explanation of our incapacity was, of course, accepted. All military organizations are alert to malingering. But suspicion runs to the malingerer himself. Malingering by order of a commanding officer is something for which the average British-trained colonel would not have been prepared.

Once the subsidy had been earned, Old Tommy went back to normal.

5

Needless to say Old Tommy used the same tactics that gave him so much satisfaction in combating tardiness and promoting military preparedness in compelling attention to academic duty. Here they were not entirely without merit.

Terror is no longer well regarded as an instrument of statecraft. It is, of course, hard on the people principally affected. But as a practical matter it is a difficult technique to administer over any period of time. A terrorist is, more or less by definition, lacking in popular appeal. And he must delegate to a rather sanguinary and unscrupulous class of subordinate. He faces in consequence the ever-recurrent danger that the executioners to whom he has delegated authority will ally themselves with the hostile public and put him away. This he may seek to avoid by accepting the even greater risks of involving himself with foreigners. The end comes either one way or the other. A few competent practitioners, of which

Stalin is the best modern example, have had a long run. Most others, from Robespierre to Hitler, have not been durable.

The low estate to which terror has fallen in the practice of public administration should not, however, be allowed to disguise its value as an adjunct to pedagogy. The limits to which men will go to avoid thought have been duly emphasized by Voltaire. He might have observed that the young will go much farther. Since a school, at its best, is a despotism of its teachers, well-considered terror can be employed without any of the retributive dangers that counsel against its use elsewhere.

Old Tommy understood this or, rather, had simply arrived at the right position. He sought to inspire a measure of fear in all his pupils; even a lad from town who could not name all of the nations and seaports from Shanghai around to Rangoon (while Old Tommy followed in the book) could expect a rebuke. For the offspring of the Scotch Old Tommy reserved the torrents of his wrath plus a virtuoso employment of eye and mustache. We quaked in fear but we struggled to learn. As a result our progress was better than might be expected and much superior to that of the children of the town. As a purely personal matter, I remain permanently grateful to Old Tommy, less for what I learned than for introducing me to a pedagogical technique that I have found endlessly useful. Only in rare instances do Harvard students put forth their best efforts in hope of reward. It is the prospect of disaster that stimulates them; graduate students in particular always distribute their surprisingly scarce energies between their classes and seminars in accordance with a close calculation of where the greatest disaster can occur. This ultimately was Old Tommy's lesson.

Tommy was not in all respects an able administrator of terror. It requires a firm intelligence to separate indifferent effort from hopeless incapacity. The first must be punished; the second has to be tolerated in such fashion that the non-achievement of the incapable does not become a precedent for others. The temptation to resort to idle threat must also be resisted. In all of these respects Old Tommy was deficient. As a result the brighter individuals eventually learned, as it was said, that you didn't need to be afraid of the Old Fart. This was deeply damaging to morale. If terror is used it must be real.

From time to time there were complaints about Old Tommy. A few of the townspeople must have suspected that he was a remarkably ignorant man. Once in the early part of the century there was, I believe, a successful movement to dislodge him. He left for a short period but his partisans brought him back. In the nature of the case most of the complaints against him came from the countryside and were discounted. And there were not too many of these; the Scotch were handicapped by the belief that learning was not meant to be painless and the line between a stern taskmaster and a mere bully is not an easy one to draw. Along with education, quite a few industrial and military careers have been made in the penumbra between the two. Old Tommy continued in office to a generous age. In the end he may conceivably have acquired for some the sentimental image of a Mr. Chips. But it couldn't have been for many.

XIII

L'Envoi

The Scotch thought well of the countryside which they inhabited. Unlike people who live on Manhattan or in South Dakota they never questioned the fate that had put them there. Only once were they afflicted with restlessness. Around the turn of the century word circulated of the spacious opportunities in the Canadian West. On every other road someone pulled up stakes, meaning that he sold his farm or surrendered his claim on the family land to his brothers and sisters, and departed for Manitoba. The Canadian railroads accommodated him in a colonist car. This was a coach fitted with slat seats and potbellied stoves in which families could camp for a few days and cook their food while they moved at some twenty miles an hour through the myriad of lakes, rocks, pine trees and insects of the Pre-Cambrian shield.

The Scotch were proud of being the descendants of pioneers. At political meetings, on St. Andrew's Day, in sermons, in homilies for the children at the Christmas concert and even in conversation the intellectual and moral leaders reminded themselves and others of the fortitude of men and women who had left the Highlands to make their way in this strange land and of the legacy of strength and courage which they had left to their children and grand-children. A community of livestock breeders has an almost instinctive understanding of genetics so it was easy to speak of the natural selection which had characterized this movement. The rugged and enterprising had come; the rest had remained behind.

However further movement was thought to be controlled by somewhat different principles. Although some of the best clans contributed to the westward movement, it was the more unsettled and frivolous members who departed. Word circulated of the violent and inhospitable country to which they had gone. It was hot in the summer and in the winter the blizzards swept across the prairie with stunning force. Sometimes the thermometer in Winnipeg went to thirty below. There were drought, grasshoppers and wheat rust. There were few trees. To depend on one crop, wheat, was perilous. There was no work in the winter. One could readily see why only the more feckless elements had been attracted. For a long while after they had gone it was supposed that one day they would be back again and fairly sheepish at that.

2

In the years following World War II the eyes of the community were again drawn to the west – this time to Detroit a mere hundred miles distant on the Michigan Central. It came to be known that a man could there make more money in three or four months than he might see in Dunwich in a year. The boys from the villages were strongly attracted. They went to Windsor and crossed the border – it was a matter of principle that this be done illegally for the United States immigration laws which interfered with access to high wages and the Canadian customs which interfered with procurement of cheap cigarettes were both considered affronts to basic human rights. On Saturday evenings these pioneers returned to Dutton wearing well-polished yellow oxfords, balloon trousers, brilliantly conceived neckties from J.L. Hudson's and, occasionally, a very high pile felt hat also of imaginative color. One girl from near the Lake also went and after serving initially as a stenographer set up as a prostitute on Woodward Avenue. She also came back for occasional weekends and wore her working clothes to Dutton on Saturday night. They emphasized vigorous magenta and violet combined with a cloche hat. Everyone was much impressed by the way she had learned to wiggle her fanny and swing her handbag. Out of respect for her parents, neighbors and their children, so it was said, she scrupulously suspended practice when she came home. But again it was a question, especially after Detroit, whether she could have thought it much of a market.

The somber social histories of Detroit of the period tell of the working man as a helpless automaton on the assembly line. All power belonged to the adamant, ruthless and heartless motor magnates. I have always wondered about this. Our Dutton boys liked their work, were fascinated by their surroundings, debated ardently the comparative merits of Fisher Body and Briggs, both of which they considered to be extensive, and were profound admirers of Henry Ford. Unless they have changed they must be a heavy trial to Walter Reuther.

3

The consequence of its epistlers was that Detroit in our community had an aura far outshining that of Toronto, Montreal, New York, Washington, London or Rome and rivaling that of Paris which was saved only by some accounts of intricately imaginative fornication that were brought back by one or two survivors of World War I. The Scotch were not wholly unaffected. A few tried the automobile factories for a winter. But no one from the prestigious clans was attracted and nearly all of the others had misgivings about working indoors and the news that one might spend the whole day hanging one door on a Ford. There was a more important reason for resisting the lure. It was, very simply, a mark of stability and intelligence to stay home and people did not wish to jeopardize their reputation for good sense.

The community was more tolerant of those who went to Toronto, London or (as had been common in earlier times) Ann Arbor for education. But while there was no open criticism of those who went, superior wisdom was thought to reside with those who remained behind. In the autumn of

1960 after some thirty years of, by the standards of the community, rather footloose activity, I interrupted a political tour in Michigan to be a guest at the Wallacetown Fair and attend a gathering of the Clan. The congressional candidate in whose district I had spoken the day before knew he wasn't going to win so he flew me in his plane to an abandoned airstrip not far from the fairgrounds. After we crossed the Detroit River we could see the glistening blue of the lakes both north and south. The country was green and golden; when we landed there was a slight smoky haze. The fair seemed much as before except for some little tykes who were racing tiny homemade automobiles. Everyone recognized me for we were the tallest of all the clans. Most asked me whether, in my travels, I had found a place as good as this. I said no for this could have been the truth and, when I faced up to it, I found I did not wish to have people think me irresponsible.

Afterword

Reading these pages again, and especially this last chapter, I think I have insufficiently emphasized the good fortune of the world that, not without some evident affection I hope, I have here described. Certainly it was a wonderful reward that it accorded those who came to it. To contend with the forests there unquestionably required a generation or two of demanding toil. (My great-grandfather seems to have succumbed at an early age to a falling tree.) Thereafter there were the broad fields of deep soil, free (unlike those in Vermont where I have long passed my summers) of stones and even more intractable ledges, and soon there were pleasant and, certainly by all modern standards, spacious houses. And schools and churches and astonishing freedom from social conflict or tension. Thomas Talbot certainly hoped he might be a landlord in the manner of Ireland, the Old World generally and the Central America of modern times, with all the envy, bitterness and anger accruing thereto. It was a fleeting dream; given the people, the land and its abundance, he never had a chance. In two or three generations not many of the Scotch in Elgin County would have exchanged places – or living standards – with those landed families who, in the Clearances, had forced their movement to the New World. Much has rightly been made of the courage and vigor of those who made and survived the initial journey into the wilderness. Less is made of the good fortune they or their children enjoyed after a few decades – or of the even greater talent for privation and suffering that was required of those who stayed behind.

Once, some fifteen or more years ago, I had occasion to make this point. Scottish Television asked me to come to the Highlands – to the land west of Loch Lomond along the Crinan Canal, whence the Galbraiths came. There would be a documentary on the return of a native son.

It was a cloudy, moist, windy day, an exceptionally unpleasant passage in early spring. The hills and their unkempt and ragged vegetation had an aspect of despair. We went to a cemetery where the Galbraiths are interred; sentiment got badly out of hand when I was asked for the camera to pick some snowdrops off a grave and give them thoughtfully to my wife. The rain and the wind got worse; the hills looked more unappealing than ever. There are some parts of Scotland, the Lowlands in particular, that are as bountiful and beautiful as any lands on earth. Not here and not on that day. At Crinan, where eventually we arrived, I had a small press conference. A reporter from the *Glasgow Herald* began the proceedings with an adequately predictable question:

"Professor Galbraith, what do you think of this country your ancestors left?"

There is a time to live and a time to die and a time when misery forces the truth. "It is impossible to believe," I replied with unforgiving emphasis, "that my ancestors made a mistake!" Next day the *Herald* told of the occasion under the headline "A Cold Wind at Crinan."

I do not believe that my children and grandchildren returning to the Lake Erie shores from wherever they now reside will have a similar response. Neither the scene nor the farmers may be thought of surpassing beauty. But none of my offspring will be moved to say, as was I, that the decision of their ancestor to depart was an act of wisdom.